To the men—
The ones answering destiny's call, drawn back to the Father's heart. To the sons, warriors, and kings in the making—this is for you. For those choosing to heal over hiding, surrender over striving. You were not made to survive—you were born to reign with honour, humility, and holy fire.

To my children—
Mighty men of courage and integrity surround you, intentionally planted by your Father. May their lives anchor you in truth and identity. You carry a legacy authored by Heaven—walk in it boldly, with reverence and joy.

This book is for the restoration of kings.
May the King of Glory be enthroned in your heart and His reign be remembered through your life.

A true king leads not by power but by the depth of his surrender and obedience to God. His authority is rooted in service, his strength in humility, and his legacy is measured by the lives he uplifts. Just as Christ reigned through love and sacrifice, so does a man walk in true kingship when he lays down his life to elevate others.

KING
YOUR CALL TO RISE

ANKE MOSTERT

Copyright © 2025

by Anke Mostert

All rights reserved. No part of this book may be reproduced, stored in a retrieval system, or transmitted in any form or by any means—electronic, mechanical, photocopying, recording, or otherwise—without prior written permission from the author, except in the case of brief quotations embodied in critical articles or reviews.

Scripture quotations used in this publication are drawn from various Bible translations, primarily from the NIV, ESV, and NKJV. All such excerpts are used solely for illustrative, educational, or contextual purposes. Using these translations does not imply endorsement of any particular version by the author, nor should it be interpreted as an official approval or affiliation with the publishers or copyright holders of the respective translations.

Original copyright holders fully retain all rights to the quoted Scripture texts. The author makes no claim of ownership over any copyrighted Bible translation cited herein. The author assumes no responsibility or liability for how readers interpret or apply the content of this book.

Published by: Crowned With Purpose (Pty) Ltd

ISBN: 978-1-0370602-7-4

For inquiries and bookings:
+27 72 206 7828
crownedwithpurposeza@gmail.com

PRINT ON DEMAND

Cape Town, South Africa

CONTENTS

1. WAR ON MAN'S IDENTITY 1
2. WOUNDS THAT KEEP MEN ASLEEP 7
3. CRISIS OF BROTHERHOOD 13
4. MIRROR OF SELF-REFLECTION 18
5. TURNING WOUNDS INTO TESTIMONIES 25
6. VICTIM TO OVERCOMER 32
7. IDENTITY IN CHRIST 38
8. SPIRITUAL DISCIPLINE 46
9. POWER OF A KING'S WORDS 52
10. STANDING IN AUTHORITY, WALKING IN HUMILITY 58
11. DECISION-MAKING 63
12. KINGDOM FINANCES 68
13. HONOURING THE TEMPLE 75
14. WHOLESOME HOBBIES AND ENTERTAINMENT 80
15. DATING LIKE A KING 85
16. SEXUAL PURITY 92
17. KING, PRIEST & HEAD OF THE HOME 99
18. FATHERHOOD IS YOUR LEGACY 104
19. RESOLVING CONFLICT 109
20. THE REFINER'S FIRE 115
21. ACCOUNTABILITY & GROWTH 119
22. LEADING AND SERVING IN THE MARKETPLACE 125
23. SERVING COMMUNITIES 130
24. GO FORTH AND CONQUER IN CHRIST'S AUTHORITY 136

FOREWORD

There comes a point in every man's journey where he must pause, look in the mirror, and confront the silent questions echoing in his soul. He feels the tug-of-war between who he pretends to be and who he might become. Underneath work routines, household tasks, and fleeting thrills, an internal voice whispers, "You were made for more." But too many men silence that voice, unsure where it leads.

This book addresses that greater calling—a call rooted in biblical truth that you have an identity infinitely more profound than your paycheque or the list of tasks you complete daily. You were designed to walk in authority, yet many men live as though they have no real impact on the world around them. Perhaps you've felt stuck, addicted, or numbly drifting through life. You may wonder if genuine transformation is possible or if these "motivational talks" are just another promise that never comes true. I invite you to keep reading to discover how an uncomplicated, yet powerful truth can change your story.

Though this book doesn't condemn or shame, it *does* sound like a clarion call: for men to reclaim their kingly position within God's design. Without men rising under Christ's authority as the head and stepping into their God-given roles, the very structure of His order begins to falter.

When you open Scripture, you see an unmistakable pattern: God created men to lead, protect, build, and steward. From Adam, endowed with dominion over creation, to the apostle Peter, entrusted with feeding and guiding Christ's flock, there's a consistent message—God entrusts men with purposeful authority. Unfortunately, many men have absorbed the lie that they have no authority or that authority is inherently oppressive. Men fear stepping up because they don't want to hurt others or doubt they have what it takes. The result is a generation of men hesitant to claim their God-given role—drifting, restless, and often resentful.

No matter how far you've wandered or how deep your cynicism is, you can choose a different path today. That's what this book is for. We'll walk through the foundational principles of biblical manhood, exploring why God designed you with significance and how you can awaken the dormant king within. We'll look at the moments that hold men back—father wounds, old failures, unchecked fears—and find genuine hope in God's ability to heal and empower.

If you've ever opened the Bible, you might notice it doesn't downplay human flaws. David, for example, was a shepherd boy who became a warrior-king, yet he also stumbled into grave moral failings. His story shows that, despite mistakes, a man after God's heart can still rise, find forgiveness, and lead a nation. That same redeeming power is available to you. The path might be messy, but genuine growth always requires us to face the mess head-on.

Though some parts of this text may cut deep, it's not here to shame you. Instead, let it serve as a mentor or a wise friend, direct and unafraid to speak the truth, but also deeply compassionate. As you read, you might feel your heart race with excitement and discomfort. Lean into that. It often means you're on the brink of a breakthrough.

One final thought: if you approach these pages with both an open mind and an open heart, I firmly believe you'll finish this book changed from who you were at the start. Allow these words to speak to your deeper self and your conscious awareness, awakening that innate desire to become the strong, compassionate, and upright leader God intended you to be. The world is desperately crying out for men like this, and you, too, can answer that call.

Welcome to the first step of the journey. May you encounter God's power and presence in ways that exceed your expectations. May you step into the fullness of who you are, no longer content to live in the shadows of mediocrity but standing upright in the light of truth.

With unwavering expectation
Anke Mostert

INTRODUCTION

FACING THE SILENT VOID

Every man harbours a secret world of inner dialogues and unspoken battles. While you may appear confident or laid-back on the outside, a dissonance can run beneath the surface—a gnawing restlessness that asks, "Is this all there is?" You sense there might be more to your existence than rushing to meet deadlines, fulfilling family obligations, or chasing fleeting pleasures. Something in you longs to be fully alive, to stand for something that outlasts your lifespan, and to leave a legacy of real substance.

This isn't just self-help talk or shallow pep. The Bible consistently highlights that men hold a pivotal influence. When God gave Adam dominion over Eden, Adam's stewardship or lack thereof, had monumental consequences (Genesis 1–3). The same principle continues today: when men are absent or apathetic, families suffer, communities fracture, and personal destinies remain unfulfilled. You might brush off these words, thinking, "I'm just an ordinary guy." But that's the point—Scripture reveals God often uses so-called 'ordinary men' to shape history. Think of Gideon, who hid from his enemies until an angel called him a "mighty warrior" (Judges 6). Gideon didn't believe it, but the truth of God's word overruled his fearful mind. The question is: how might God's perspective overrule your self-doubt?

WHY MEN LOSE THEIR WAY

At some point, life can feel like a chaotic swirl of expectations—from family, friends, employers, society, and even our relentless inner critic. Many men shrink under these pressures and sometimes numb themselves with addictions—whether substances, entertainment, or unhealthy relationships. Others become workaholics, seeking validation in promotions and paycheques. But the deeper issue remains untouched: they have lost sight of their core identity and spiritual authority. The gravitational pull of everyday life distracts men from more significant questions like, "What is my purpose?" or "How can I truly change my sphere of influence for the better?"

Then there's the father wound. Perhaps you grew up with a distant or absent father figure, leaving you uncertain about how to be a decisive, compassionate leader. Or maybe you had a father who was physically present but emotionally cold, never offering genuine affirmation. These voids travel with you, shaping how you relate to authority, approach relationships, and ultimately view God. Too often, these wounds remain unacknowledged and unhealed.

STEPPING INTO THE GAP

God never intended for men to wander. The Scripture is filled with explicit calls for men to rise, guided by the Holy Spirit, to reclaim the influence the enemy has cunningly stolen. We see this in Nehemiah, who rebuilt Jerusalem's walls despite opposition. We see it in the apostle Paul, who mentored spiritual sons like Timothy, ensuring the next generation had a blueprint for ministry. Even Jesus recognised the weight of spiritual authority when He told Peter, "On this rock, I will build My church..." (Matthew 16:18). No man—yourself included—is exempt from a role in God's redemptive plan.

CONFRONTING YOUR BARRIERS

Before plunging into the chapters ahead, take a moment to reflect on the invisible barriers holding you back. Perhaps it's a shame over a past mistake. Maybe it's an addiction. It could even be something as subtle as cynicism, that grim voice in your head that says, "Things never really change." Those forces lose their power when exposed to the truth. The more you let the biblical foundation of your identity seep into your subconscious, the less those negative voices can dominate your life.

Expect some discomfort as we tackle sensitive issues. Real growth demands honesty about where you're stuck, where you've been hurt, or even where you've hurt others. But also expect hope. The God who called broken fishermen to become fishers of men is the same God who calls you to step out of stagnation. In the following pages, you'll find a roadmap—straightforward teaching interwoven with scriptural examples and practical guidance. Where many motivational messages leave you inspired but not anchored, this book will direct you back to the Word of God, the only unshakeable foundation.

WHAT LIES AHEAD

We'll begin by exposing the war waged against a man's identity from birth, revealing how the enemy's lies have tried to keep you bound and asleep. From there, we will confront the hidden wounds that often cripple men from within—fatherlessness, betrayal, addiction, and past failures—and invite God's healing into the deepest places of your heart. As healing takes root, we will move into reclaiming your true identity in Christ, exchanging survival for kingship and victimhood for victorious authority. Foundational principles such as spiritual discipline, decision-making, stewardship, and godly leadership will shape the blueprint for living daily as a king who both leads and serves with humility and strength.

Along the journey, you will encounter powerful biblical narratives—stories of broken, doubting, and even rebellious men who still found redemption and rose to fulfil their callings. Their victories and failures will mirror your battles, proving that genuine transformation is possible and promised to those who yield to God's refining process. Chapter by chapter, you will be equipped to stand as a man who knows his worth, guards his heart, leads with integrity, and leaves a lasting legacy. No matter how far you've fallen or how hidden your greatness feels, the King of Glory is calling you to rise.

AN INVITATION TO GO DEEPER

As you enter this book, know that the journey is more than acquiring head knowledge. It's about letting God's truth penetrate your subconscious mind. It's about dethroning the lies that have ruled your thoughts for too long. It's about catching a vision of your life when you fully align with God's plans, refusing to settle for mediocrity.

This book aims to stir an urgency within you that says, "I cannot remain how I've been." If you feel that stirring, don't push it aside. Lean into it. The restlessness you sense might be the Holy Spirit inviting you into a life of greater freedom, purpose, and impact.

READY FOR MORE?

Take a deep breath because we're about to dive in. If you feel a flutter in your chest or a lump in your throat, that's good—it means something in your spirit is awakening to possibility. Keep that anticipation alive. Let the words feed your curiosity and speak life over your doubts.

The path of kingship isn't for the faint of heart, but you're not faint of heart—you're here, ready to discover what "more" indeed looks like. And that's what we'll learn together, step by step, chapter by chapter.

Welcome to the beginning. You are not alone, nor are you powerless. There is a King who calls you by name, and He invites you to stand in the authority He's given you. Turn the page—and let the journey transform you from the inside out.

Are you ready to answer the call?

HOW TO APPROACH THIS BOOK

1. **Read with Expectation**

   Have your Bible at hand and read the quoted scriptures. Approach each chapter believing it can transform your perspective. Pray before you read, asking God to illuminate your understanding and overcome emotional walls.

2. **Engage Actively**

   As you encounter questions, take them seriously. Journal your answers, discuss them with a trusted friend, or pray through them. Passive reading rarely produces profound change.

3. **Apply, Don't Just Admire**

   It's easy to nod at good ideas and return to the same life patterns. Fundamental transformation requires practical application: changing a habit, apologising to someone, taking a step of faith, or joining a men's group for accountability.

4. **Stay Open to the Holy Spirit**

   The Holy Spirit is your greatest ally in this journey. His counsel and comfort will meet you in moments of conviction or when you revisit painful memories. Don't face these pages alone—welcome God's presence.

CHAPTER 1

WAR ON MAN'S IDENTITY

From the moment a man is conceived, the war begins. Before he takes his first breath—before his heart even beats outside the womb—the enemy has already launched his assault. This battle does not begin in adulthood nor when a man first faces temptation or hardship. It is an ancient war waged before he had the language to describe it or the awareness to resist it. The enemy's goal is clear: if he can convince a man that he was born to fail, that man will never step into his God-ordained kingship. If a man believes he is insignificant, unworthy, or powerless, he will never claim the authority that was always meant to be his.

For many men, this attack takes root in the unseen, whispered before birth through rejection, abandonment, or the sting of an unwanted conception. How many men entered the world unplanned, labelled with words like "We weren't ready for you" or "You were an accident"? These words are not harmless; they are weapons designed to plant seeds of insignificance before a boy even knows who he is. A man who grows up believing he is not wanted will spend his life searching for belonging in places that can never satisfy him.

As he enters childhood, the battle intensifies. Words from parents, teachers, and peers begin to shape his self-image. A boy who is repeatedly told, "You'll never amount to anything," begins to internalise that belief. A child whose emotions are dismissed as weakness learns to shut them down, hardening his heart to an unsafe world. A son whose father is physically or emotionally absent wrestles with the silent question: "Am I enough?" These wounds do not simply fade with time; instead, they become the script that governs a man's thoughts long after childhood has passed.

Then comes adolescence, a stage in which insecurity grips young men as they measure themselves against others, questioning their strength, intelligence, and worth. Some respond by striving—seeking validation through achievements and hoping that success will silence the inner voice telling them they are not enough. Others rebel, embracing recklessness over responsibility because failure seems inevitable. At every turn, the enemy whispers: "You are not strong enough. You are not smart enough. You are not worthy of love."

By adulthood, many men have settled for an identity of survival rather than kingship. They work, provide, and do what is expected, yet they live in quiet resignation deep down. They are convinced they were never destined for greatness. They view their past mistakes as proof of unworthiness, content to remain small—afraid to dream, afraid to lead, and afraid to embrace their divine assignment.

This deception is the enemy's most significant victory: not simply destroying a man physically but persuading him that he was never meant to reign in the first place. A man who does not know he is a king will never take dominion. A man who believes he is a failure will never fight for victory. The enemy does not need to destroy a man who voluntarily surrenders his authority.

Yet here is the truth the enemy fears: a man's identity is not determined by his circumstances of birth. Past failures, cruel words, or inflicted wounds do not define it. His identity is anchored in the One who created him. From the moment of conception, God spoke a destiny over him. He was not an accident. He was not unwanted. He was designed with a purpose, crafted with intention, and marked for kingship.

Jesus Himself was attacked at birth. As soon as His arrival was announced, King Herod sought to kill Him (Matthew 2:16). Why? Because the enemy recognised the threat He posed to the kingdom of darkness. So, it is with every man—Satan sees your potential even before you do. He knows that once you awaken to your identity, you will become a force that disrupts his agenda. He has tried to keep you blind, but the chains break when you recognise the truth.

This awakening often begins as a restless stirring, a whisper in your soul that says, "You were meant for more." You might achieve a comfortable life—paying bills, meeting obligations—but still feel an ache, a dissatisfaction that asks, "Is this all there is?" That question is not a crisis; it is a call. The same call reached

Gideon, hiding in a winepress, convinced of his insignificance. When the angel appeared, he did not address Gideon by his current condition; instead, he spoke to Gideon's true identity: "The Lord is with you, mighty warrior" (Judges 6:12). Gideon could not see himself that way, but Heaven did—and the same is true of you.

When God calls a man to step into kingship, the most significant barriers are not external but internal. Apathy convinces him that nothing grand is possible, so he may as well settle for survival. Fear whispers, "What if I fail? What if I'm not enough?" These lies chain men to mediocrity. Yet Scripture constantly reminds us: "Fear not." Fear is a liar, stealing the courage to step into your calling.

Consider David—a forgotten shepherd boy, overlooked by his father. When God sent Samuel to anoint a king, He bypassed every imposing older brother and chose David from the field. David's circumstances did not look regal, but God saw the king within him. Perhaps you have been overlooked, passed over, dismissed, or counted out. God sees beyond what human eyes perceive. He sees the king in you.

If you remain paralysed by fear or weighed down by past hurts, you will never take hold of the dominion that is already yours. But if you dare to believe you were made for more, if you reject the lies and align yourself with the truth, transformation begins. This is not about self-help or motivational hype but divine identity. A king does not wait for someone to hand him his authority—he steps forward and claims his inheritance. He walks in confidence that comes not from himself but from the One who called him.

This is your wake-up call. You were not created merely to survive. You were not meant to exist without purpose or to wander. You were born to reign. You were chosen to lead, protect, cultivate, and expand the Kingdom of God. The enemy has spent years persuading you otherwise, but the truth stands unshaken: you are a king under Christ's authority. Now is the time to rise, to silence the lies, and to reclaim what was always yours.

It does not matter how far you have strayed, how many mistakes you have made, or how many years have slipped away. God is not bound by time. He redeems, He restores, He rebuilds. The battle for your identity has raged since the moment of your conception, but this day, you choose the outcome. Will you continue under the weight of a lie, or will you step into the kingship that has been your inheritance all along?

The enemy trembles at the thought of a man who knows who he is—who knows he is called, who knows he is anointed, who knows he is a threat to the kingdom of darkness. Stand up. Shake off the deception. Step into the authority that has awaited you from the beginning. You are not here by accident. You were born to reign.

CLOSING THOUGHTS

Since you were conceived, there has been a relentless war against your identity as a man. Before you drew your first breath, the enemy sought to undermine your purpose, planting seeds of insignificance, rejection, and insecurity to keep you from realising your true kingship. These attacks, subtle yet destructive, have shaped your self-image from childhood through adulthood, convincing you to accept a life of mere survival instead of stepping into your God-ordained authority.

But your identity is not defined by your past, your wounds, or the lies whispered by the enemy. It is anchored in the powerful truth of who God says you are—a king crafted with intention, purpose, and divine authority. Your circumstances do not determine your destiny; God does. Just as He called Gideon from hiding and David from obscurity, He calls you now.

CALL TO ACTION

Today, reject the lies and break free from the chains of deception. Choose to embrace the identity God has spoken over your life. You were not born merely to exist; you were created to reign. Step boldly into your authority, claim your inheritance, and rise into the kingship that is rightfully yours. The enemy fears your awakening—so stand up, reclaim your identity, and step courageously into the destiny God has always intended for you.

CHAPTER 2

WOUNDS THAT KEEP MEN ASLEEP

Men often carry deep wounds that lie just beneath the surface, subtly shaping how they think, behave, and relate to others. Few hurts cut more profoundly than those connected to fatherhood and authority. Our first understanding of love, discipline, and affirmation is usually formed through the hands and words of our earthly fathers. When that relationship proves absent, harsh, or emotionally cold, a man grows into adulthood with a deficit—a hollow ache for validation that drives him to seek approval in places that cannot heal him.

Maybe you never heard the words "I'm proud of you," so you sought accolades at work or plunged into relationships that couldn't fill the void. Perhaps your father was missing entirely, undermining your sense of worth. Whatever its shape, the father wound bleeds into every aspect of a man's life, influencing how he sees God, loves others, and leads his home. And until that wound is acknowledged and healed, a man is unfit to exercise physical discipline over his children. Discipline without healing becomes reactionary, not redemptive, an outlet for unresolved pain rather than an act of love. A man still bleeding cannot guide his children with clarity or compassion. His healing is not optional but essential for his freedom and the legacy he will leave behind.

The Bible offers a potent picture of how these wounds can fester. Jacob favoured his son Joseph above the others (Genesis 37), stirring deep jealousy and bitterness among his brothers. Feeling invisible and unloved, they betrayed Joseph, selling him into slavery. Their shared wound sprang from a father's misplaced affection, unleashing a cycle of envy and hurt. While your experience may not be as extreme, the principle stands: when a father's role is undercut—through absence, neglect, or partiality—many sons grow up uncertain, resentful, or emotionally distant. That unresolved pain often seeps into marriage, parenting, or leadership, causing men to lash out or withdraw. A king unaware of his wounds risks bleeding on those he's meant to lead.

Yet father wounds aren't the only source of spiritual scar tissue. Betrayal by close friends, heartbreak in romantic relationships, or the failure of trusted leaders can also leave deep gashes in a man's soul. You might be hesitant to trust mentors or reluctant to lead, haunted by memories of broken confidence. In Peter's case, denying Jesus three times inflicted shame that could have disqualified him from apostolic leadership. But after the resurrection, Jesus purposely drew Peter aside, asking him thrice, "Do you love Me?" (John 21:15–17). Rather than condemning Peter's guilt, He healed it, restoring Peter's calling to "feed My sheep." That same grace applies to you. The wounds you bear do not have to be your downfall. If named, surrendered, and laid before God, they can become channels of redemption—a testimony that no hurt is too deep for His restoring power.

One of Scripture's most significant revelations is that we are adopted as sons by God Himself (Romans 8:15). If you grew up believing fathers were inherently cruel or indifferent, embracing God's fatherhood may feel unnatural. The more you open your heart to Him, the more you'll see a Father who loves perfectly, disciplines wisely, and never abandons. Such a realisation dismantles the lies you've internalised: "I must earn approval," "I'm inherently unworthy," or "I can't rely on anyone." God's adoption confers a new status. In Him, you are not a cast-off but a beloved child—a truth that rips apart the shame and confusion left by earthly wounds.

Healing starts with naming the hurt. Whether it's fatherlessness, betrayal, or a general sense of rejection, call it what it is. Journaling can bring needed clarity. From there, surrender the wound to God. Invite Him into that vulnerable space: "Lord, I bring You my hurt—heal me, show me who I am in You." Often, we need a supportive community to walk this out, whether it's a trusted pastor, counsellor, or men's group where others can speak life and remind us we're not alone. Forgiveness plays an enormous role as well. It doesn't absolve the offender of responsibility, but it frees you from carrying anger or bitterness that only prolongs the wound. Finally, affirmations from Scripture—"I am chosen, I am loved, I am called" (Ephesians 1:4–5, 1 Peter 2:9)—renew your mind, replacing negative self-talk with God's perspective.

Remarkably, the place of your deepest pain can become where God's grace shines brightest. In 2 Corinthians 12:9, He tells Paul, "My power is made perfect in weakness." The scars you've hidden can be doorways to a more profound walk with the Father. Imagine rising from your father wound or betrayal not defeated, but transformed—carrying greater wisdom, deeper kindness, and a sharper sensitivity to the pain others carry. That redemption story enriches every aspect of your kingship, allowing you to empathise rather than judge, to nurture rather than dominate. You lead differently when you lead from a place of being healed. Instead of insecurity or anger, you operate with compassion, giving your spouse, children, or community the best version of the man God intended you to be.

It may feel daunting to excavate these old hurts. Yet, consider Peter's transformation after Christ dealt directly with his shame. Upon receiving grace, Peter became a pillar of the early Church, bold enough to preach to thousands at Pentecost. Joseph, once a wounded younger brother sold into slavery, rose to govern Egypt and save nations from famine. Wounds do not have to derail your destiny. Instead, when surrendered to God, they can catapult you into your calling with greater empathy and fortitude. Pain that once threatened to keep you asleep can awaken you to your God-given dominion, recharging your sense of purpose and enabling you to lead from a heart that has encountered divine love.

So let this chapter be your invitation to face the hidden injuries you've grown accustomed to carrying. Reflect on where they originated—an absent father, broken trust, or a deep personal betrayal. Speak these wounds aloud in prayer, confessing the toll they've taken. Seek out the supportive presence of godly men or mentors who have navigated similar paths. Dare to forgive those who harmed you, releasing them into God's hands while protecting your heart from bitterness. And above all, open yourself to the Father's unwavering affection. Let His words, "You are My beloved son," (Mark 1:11) sink deep enough to dislodge the lies you've believed about yourself.

In doing so, you transform the very wounds meant to debilitate you into sources of renewed faith, clarity, and leadership. You become the king who knows he's deeply loved, leading others from a place of security, not striving. You become the father who breaks destructive cycles, offering your children or spiritual sons a kinder, healthier model of love. You become the husband or friend who invests in relationships without the baggage of unresolved pain. And you become the man who lives fully awake, free from the shackles of past hurts, ready to shape the world around you with grace-filled authority.

CLOSING THOUGHTS

Many men bear hidden emotional wounds, often stemming from broken relationships with fathers, experiences of betrayal, or feelings of rejection. These wounds quietly shape a man's identity, influence relationships, and impact his leadership abilities. God invites each man to face and heal these painful places. By courageously acknowledging, surrendering, and forgiving past hurts, you allow God's transformative grace to reshape your pain into a powerful source of compassion, wisdom, and strength.

CALL TO ACTION

Now is the moment to bravely confront the hidden wounds you've carried for far too long. Identify the root causes of your pain, express them openly through prayer and reflection, and surrender these hurts to God's healing embrace. Connect with supportive mentors or trusted friends who can journey alongside you. Commit to forgiveness, embracing your true identity as a cherished son of God. Step forward into a renewed, empowered life, leading with authenticity, confidence, and grace from the deep wells of healing you've experienced.

CHAPTER 3

CRISIS OF BROTHERHOOD

When we think of betrayal, we often envision treacherous acts—deception, theft, or outright disloyalty. Yet among men, the most insidious betrayals are not those of action but of inaction. They manifest in silent approval, in the refusal to challenge another's descent into ruin. Consider a man who hints at his growing addiction or the unravelling of his marriage. Rather than confront him, you offer a sympathetic nod and turn away. Too often, such indifference is the quiet force that ushers men to their downfall, as those closest to them choose ease over duty. True brotherhood is not passive; it demands intervention. To ignore a man's faltering steps is to leave him alone in his struggle, no matter how many voices call him friend. The Bible urges men to stay vigilant in their associations, declaring blessing over the one who refuses to walk with the wicked, stand with sinners, or sit amongst mockers (Psalm 1:1).

One of the earliest biblical portrayals of this problem appears in Genesis 4, when Cain defiantly asks God, "Am I my brother's keeper?" In ignoring Abel's welfare, Cain displays a callousness that ultimately leads to tragedy. We may not physically harm one another as he did, but by neglecting a friend who's falling apart, we can inadvertently kill his potential or erode his hope. Men frequently maintain surface-level relationships—bonding over sports, shared hobbies, or casual jokes—while significant emotional and spiritual battles simmer beneath the facade. Even when we sense a friend is in trouble, we shy away, concerned we might intrude on personal matters or assume someone else will intervene.

Yet real friendship, the kind that can save a life or a future, requires more. It insists we speak truth lovingly, even if doing so is uncomfortable. Jonathan showed this commitment when he aided David (1 Samuel 18–20). Despite the danger King Saul presented, Jonathan took risks to protect David, refusing to remain silent. Brotherhood implies the willingness to get involved—driving a friend to see a counsellor or confronting him if he drifts toward destructive choices. Genuine accountability means calling out issues before they escalate, which might involve urging him to join a small group for support or to adopt accountability software if pornography has become an unspoken battle.

These deeper connections do not emerge spontaneously. Men rarely bare their souls without invitation. Breaking the code of silence demands someone go first, volunteering vulnerability that opens the door for reciprocal honesty. Creating consistent ground rules—whether in a weekly men's gathering or a simple three-man accountability circle—helps cultivate an environment of trust. Imagine a setting where no topic is off-limits and no concern is dismissed. That kind of circle doesn't stop at sympathy; it encourages practical steps toward healing. Instead of leaving a friend adrift, it checks in repeatedly, providing tangible support.

Scripture offers another powerful illustration of proactive brotherhood in Barnabas, which means "Son of Encouragement". When many believers distrusted Paul's conversion, Barnabas vouched for him (Acts 9:26–27). Later, he travelled with Paul on missionary journeys, fuelling his growth and ministry potential. If Barnabas had played it safe, Paul might have floundered indefinitely. Often, we behave like onlookers, cautious about involving ourselves in another man's struggles. But a Barnabas invests real energy—time, prayer, resources—to ensure a friend's hidden greatness is not lost.

We live in a culture that portrays men as proud, stoic, or detached from emotional needs. That stereotype must be dismantled by intentionally demonstrating deeper accountability. In our families, we show authenticity by acknowledging our mistakes and striving to amend them because of our children. With our peers, we move conversations beyond light banter, pressing into spiritual questions, mental well-being, or relationship challenges. And in our wider community—church, sports clubs, workplaces—we become mentors to younger men who desperately need a model of honourable masculinity.

Neglecting this calling can be fatal. We see men quietly battling depression, addiction, or a breakdown in relationships, all the while receiving only superficial nods of understanding from friends who remain uninvolved. A friend's crisis won't solve itself without someone willing to push through discomfort. Whether Jonathan opposes Saul for David's sake or Barnabas advocates for Paul, real brotherhood must choose inconvenient loyalty over passive detachment.

So reflect: Are there men in your circle slipping into harmful choices or emotional ruts, subtly crying out for help? Have you let a quick "That's rough" be your only response? Brotherhood is not about moral superiority but about caring enough to save a fellow man from stumbling further. "Speaking the truth in love" (Ephesians 4:15) calls for compassion and conviction. A band of brothers forged by such commitment replaces a culture of shallow talk with transformative fellowship—one that can rescue a friend's marriage, preserve his calling, or rekindle a lost sense of purpose. This is how men sharpen one another, becoming genuine keepers of each other's potential and well-being as God intended.

CLOSING THOUGHTS

The actual crisis of brotherhood isn't obvious betrayal but silent indifference. When men choose comfort or passivity over courageous intervention—whether facing a friend's addiction, marital collapse, or emotional despair—they quietly become accomplices to his downfall, leaving them isolated in their struggles. Real brotherhood is uncomfortable; it demands heartfelt honesty, confronting harmful patterns, and demonstrating tangible support. Like Jonathan protecting David or Barnabas advocating for Paul, authentic brotherhood requires vulnerability, risk, and deep intentionality. Only through proactive involvement and honest commitment can men sharpen, heal, and uplift one another, becoming genuine guardians of each other's lives and destinies.

CALL TO ACTION

Right now, picture a man in your life who's quietly slipping toward crisis—a friend needing more than your sympathetic nod. Refuse to stay passive. Break the silence today. Reach out, initiate an honest conversation, and offer tangible support. Brotherhood isn't built by good intentions; it's forged through courageous actions. His future—and yours—may depend on it. Restoring accountability among men begins with you.

CHAPTER 4

MIRROR OF SELF-REFLECTION

Before fully embracing your identity in Christ, you must examine how you perceive yourself—spiritually and physically. How you see yourself often determines how you live, and your spiritual stance sets the tone for everything that follows in the physical realm. This act of self-reflection is more than simple introspection; it is a mirror designed to reveal the lens through which you view your worth, abilities, and purpose. When you pause long enough to take stock of who you are and how you see yourself, you identify the beliefs, wounds, and aspirations guiding your choices. Only then can you invite God to reshape them according to His truth.

From a spiritual vantage point, self-reflection asks, "What do I truly believe about God, and what do I believe about how He sees me?" Scripture teaches that we are created in the image of God (Genesis 1:27), destined for meaningful fellowship with Him. Yet it is easy to carry distorted views of self—perhaps inherited from painful childhood experiences, repeated failures, or culture's contradictory voices. Even men who faithfully attend church can drift into a mindset defined by shame or insecurity, uncertain if God cares about their everyday struggles. Rather than living as beloved sons, they settle for feeling tolerated by a distant deity. If your internal narrative says, "I am inadequate" or "I am inherently flawed," you filter all of life through that defeat. Part of self-reflection is pinpointing these defeating assumptions and questioning them in the light of Scripture.

Equally significant is acknowledging the physical stance that flows from your spiritual one. If you believe you are unloved or stuck in a cycle of failure, you may stop caring about your body, appearance, or habits. A man who views himself as worthless might adopt unhealthy extremes—laziness, overindulgence, or neglect of personal presentation. Conversely, a man who sees his body as a temple (1 Corinthians 6:19) finds motivation to responsibly steward his health, posture, and lifestyle. When you perceive your worth through God's eyes—treasured, chosen, and purposed—you naturally begin to live with integrity in the physical realm. You walk taller, speak more confidently, and treat your body respectfully, knowing it is a vessel for God's work.

Yet self-reflection requires courage because it often confronts uncomfortable truths. You may discover you have relied on substances, busyness or surface-level success to avoid addressing a greater spiritual emptiness. Or perhaps you have let negative voices convince you that you have no value, leading to hopelessness in your physical health or daily habits. This confrontation can feel like standing in front of a glaring mirror, every flaw illuminated. But God does not reveal our broken parts to shame us—He reveals the broken parts so that healing and transformation can begin. Psalm 139:23–24 cries, "Search me, O God, and know my heart... see if there is any offensive way in me and lead me in the way everlasting." By inviting God's Spirit to search your inner life, you step onto the road of restoration, where every falsehood about who you are is replaced by divine truth.

Practically, setting aside time for honest evaluation is key. Find a quiet place to reflect and pray or even to journal about your current feelings, attitudes, and habits. Ask yourself: "How do I view my spiritual life, and what do I believe about God's character?" "Do I see myself as loved, or am I still striving for acceptance?" "Am I stewarding my physical body in a way that honours God, or have I let discouragement and excuses dictate my health choices?" This process may surface regrets, fears, or even sins you have swept under the rug. It also may uncover hidden aspirations—dreams and callings you put on hold because you felt unworthy. Self-reflection is not designed to wallow in negativity; it is meant to highlight your potential and show the gap between who you are now and who God created you to be.

In this internal inventory, be prepared to meet God's grace. Where you are weary or broken, He offers renewal (Isaiah 40:31). Where you cling to shame, He extends forgiveness (1 John 1:9). Where you feel powerless, He reminds you that His strength is made perfect in weakness (2 Corinthians 12:9). Embracing grace is not an excuse to remain passive but a catalyst to change. Once you see yourself through Heaven's lens, you gain the motivation to transform your daily lifestyle, be it discipline in your diet and exercise, responsibility in your finances, or diligence in your work ethic. A man who aligns his physical stance with his spiritual convictions discovers consistency—his interior beliefs match how he carries himself in the world.

Moreover, self-reflection is not a solitary pursuit. Sharing your discoveries with a trusted friend, mentor, or brother in Christ can help keep you accountable. Conversations in a safe community can confirm the truths God speaks to your heart while revealing blind spots you might miss. Sometimes, an external voice can affirm your overlooked qualities or gently correct the patterns you have rationalised. When you place your reflections in the context of fellowship, you increase your likelihood of genuine transformation. You move beyond personal insights into communal support, which is invaluable for lasting change.

Eventually, this reflection chapter becomes the gateway to a more profound revelation about your identity in Christ. By probing your spiritual and physical stances, you dismantle illusions, clarify your motivations, and lay a foundation to support new growth. Should you choose to remain ignorant of how you currently view yourself, any further teaching on kingship risks becoming academic rather than transformative. After all, a man cannot fully step into the role of a king if he perceives himself as a perpetual victim, nor can he effectively govern his sphere if he refuses to acknowledge the baggage he carries. When the illusions fall, you can hear God's call more clearly—an invitation to reign with Him, secure in who you are, and free to reflect His presence in every aspect of life.

So let this moment of self-reflection be an act of faith, trusting that God meets you in your reality and guides you toward wholeness. By confronting your internal narratives and outward habits, you prepare the soil of your heart for seeds of identity to flourish. Soon, you will delve into understanding your identity in Christ, a vital next step. But that seed needs fertile ground—a heart made honest before God and open to transformation. Start by seeing yourself clearly, then watch God reshape you according to His design, bridging the gap between who you've been and who you are destined to become.

CLOSING THOUGHTS

True kingship begins with courageous and honest self-reflection—seeing yourself clearly and honestly through God's spiritual and physical perspective. It requires acknowledging the strengths and potential He has placed within you and confronting the areas where false beliefs, unhealthy habits, or distorted views have taken root. By intentionally examining your inner narratives, spiritual convictions, and outward behaviours, you can begin to identify and challenge the misconceptions holding you back from your divine calling. This deep and honest reflection enables you to replace falsehoods with the life-giving truths in Scripture, empowering you to align every aspect of your life with God's purposes. As you do this work, you lay a solid foundation for authentic transformation and begin to embody your true identity as a king in Christ.

CALL TO ACTION

Commit today to the essential practice of intentional self-reflection. Dedicate specific, undistracted time during this week for prayerful contemplation and journaling using the reflective questions provided in this chapter. Allow yourself to explore your beliefs about God, your self-worth, physical health, and daily habits. Invite God to gently reveal areas of your heart and life needing His healing and transformation. Then, courageously share your discoveries with a trusted friend, mentor, or brother in Christ who can offer support, accountability, and encouragement on your journey. Remember, genuine growth occurs when insights move beyond awareness into tangible action. Embrace this critical step wholeheartedly, preparing yourself to live out the kingship God has designed for you.

CHAPTER 5

TURNING WOUNDS INTO TESTIMONIES

A king who bears unhealed wounds remains a captive, unable to walk in the fullness of his God-given authority. Emotional and spiritual wounds shape our thoughts, influence our reactions, and often define how we lead. When we neglect these injuries—whether caused by fatherlessness, betrayal, failure, or unresolved trauma—we risk carrying them as open sores that weaken our ability to serve, love, and advance God's Kingdom. Unresolved pain, like an undrained wound, undermines our spiritual zeal and relational stability. It robs us of the freedom and clarity essential for genuine leadership.

On the other hand, healing is the process by which our wounds no longer remain raw but turn into scars—visible reminders of where we have been, yet no longer places of ongoing pain. While scars do not vanish, they can become testimonies of grace rather than points of defeat. The Scriptures showcase this truth repeatedly. Consider Joseph's betrayal by his brothers and subsequent years in slavery and prison (Genesis 37–50). He could have grown bitter, letting his wounds define him. Instead, Joseph allowed God to transform that hurt into wisdom and maturity.

When elevated to second in command over Egypt, he saved nations from famine and forgave the people who had wronged him. His scar became his story of redemption, a living testimony that God can bring good out of evil.

One of the most significant barriers to healing is the tendency to look back and remain stuck. Many men replay their past—failures, shame, regrets, or deep-seated wounds—like a broken record in their minds. They become prisoners to that moment of pain, never moving forward. Yet the Bible consistently reminds us not to dwell on "former things" (Isaiah 43:18–19). This is not because the past lacks significance but because God's plan for us is progressive. We cannot effectively receive new blessings or march forward in authority when our gaze is locked on old defeats. Healing does not ignore the past—it confronts it. But once confronted and surrendered to God, we do not linger there; we transition to wholeness.

Without healing, a king's perspective is skewed. Anger, bitterness, shame, or fear from unhealed wounds can distort decision-making, poison relationships, and undermine even the best intentions. The pain seeps into how we speak to our spouses, handle conflict, or mentor others. Wounded men often seek solace in addictions, distractions, or destructive patterns, wasting years and opportunities in cycles of avoidance. Tragically, these cycles do more than hurt the wounded man—they affect families, friends, workplaces, and entire communities. A man who refuses to heal risks spreading the infection of his hurt to every realm he is called to oversee.

Healing, therefore, is essential for stepping into a robust kingship. A man who has allowed God to tend to his deepest wounds emerges not weakened but strengthened—grounded in empathy for others, confident in God's grace, and bold in the knowledge that God redeems what once seemed hopeless. Jesus Himself offers to lift the burden of past pains (Matthew 11:28–30). He does not merely apply a temporary bandage; He leads us into wholeness. This is no quick fix, but a journey involving prayer, sometimes counselling, genuine repentance where needed, and forgiveness—often extended to those who never apologised. This process can feel uneasy, even painful, but it transforms us from the inside out, enabling us to rule over our emotions rather than be ruled by them.

Only when we heal can we effectively testify to God's redemptive power. A scar testifies that a wound happened, and yes, it hurt—but it is closed now. It is no longer a site of agony but a symbol that God's grace has triumphed. Scars can become tools for ministry: the fatherless man who found his identity in Christ now mentors boys without fathers, the recovering addict who overcame bondage becomes a voice of hope to others, or the betrayed husband who chose to forgive helps other couples facing heartbreak. These men do not bury their histories; they harness them, bearing witness that God meets us in the valley and leads us onto the mountaintop of recovery.

The reward of healing is wholeness: a heart unencumbered by bitterness or shame, a mind able to see opportunities instead of reeling from old betrayals, and relationships that flourish because you no longer bristle with unspoken resentments. Wholeness does not mean perfection. Instead, it means nothing stands in the way of you and God—no hidden grudges, no crippling regrets—and thus, nothing stands in the way of you stepping into your kingly mandate. Where you once may have projected anger, you now project compassion. Where you once guarded yourself with cynicism, you now lead with confident vulnerability. Such transformation does not happen overnight, but every step toward healing reclaims territory that once belonged to pain.

We must choose to partner with God in the healing process. This means inviting the Holy Spirit to search our hearts for buried hurts, acknowledging them openly, and surrendering them to Him in prayer. Some men find that journaling or confiding in a trusted mentor reveals layers of hurt that they never realised shaped their daily lives. Others might need to go through structured inner healing prayer, counselling, or dedicated fasting times to break patterns of shame or anger. Each man's path to healing will look different, but the common thread is submission to God's method and timing. Patience is crucial, for deep wounds often require deep work. Each scar becomes a testament to God's faithfulness as healing progresses, forging greater compassion and sharper discernment in your leadership style.

When you heal, you do more than lighten your load—you expand your capacity to serve. A healed king leads from a place of empathy, not suspicion. Other people's brokenness does not threaten him because he knows that brokenness can be restored. He does not fear conflict or vulnerability, having walked through his pain to the other side. People naturally trust a man who has overcome adversity and is now transparent about God's role in his victory. Your personal story of healing can open countless doors for ministry, encouragement, and the building of God's Kingdom. Simply put, a wounded king hides behind defences, but a healed king steps forward with open arms, inviting others into the redemption he has experienced.

Therefore, decide to heal rather than stagnate. Stop replaying the wound in your mind and yield it to the One who will transform it into a testimony of grace. Forgive where you must, repent where necessary, grieve if needed—but do not remain stuck. If your life feels overshadowed by a recurring hurt, let this be the day you seek the healing presence of Christ. A king is not defined by his scars but by how he allows God to use them for good. As those scars shift from markers of injury to markers of resurrection power, you will find the unstoppable momentum of a man released from his chains—a man ready to reign as God intended.

In the end, healing does not erase your scars; it redefines them. You do not lose your story, but your story loses its power to enslave you. Instead, it becomes a reservoir of wisdom and compassion that blesses others. This is the gift of wholeness for the king in Christ: every pain redeemed, every tear answered, every disappointment overshadowed by a more significant promise. Having walked through the fire of suffering, you emerge refined, a living testament to the God who binds the brokenhearted and sets the captives free. That is the beauty of healing: it takes what once threatened to ruin you and transforms it into an eternal testimony of God's grace, propelling you into your rightful kingship with more faith, empathy, and authority than ever.

CLOSING THOUGHTS

In summary, healing transforms your wounds from sources of pain into testimonies of divine grace. Unresolved wounds can trap a king in cycles of bitterness and defeat, impacting every aspect of life and leadership. Yet when you courageously partner with God to address these wounds—through forgiveness, repentance, and authentic surrender—you exchange chains for freedom, bitterness for compassion, and hurt for powerful ministry. Your scars no longer define you; they become tools in God's hands, empowering your leadership and inspiring others toward their healing journeys.

CALL TO ACTION

Today, choose to break free from the chains of past wounds. Reflect honestly: What hurt or resentment has been left untreated in your heart? Invite God's healing touch into those places. Reach out to a mentor, journal your prayers, pursue counselling, or engage in intentional fasting and prayer. Do not remain captive any longer. Your scars await transformation into testimonies that declare God's power and grace. Step forward boldly—your kingship depends on it.

CHAPTER 6

VICTIM TO OVERCOMER

In life's journey, circumstances can sometimes overshadow our sense of power and purpose. Men who endure repeated disappointments—whether rooted in childhood wounds, failed ventures, or complex relationships—may begin to see themselves as victims of life rather than participants in a divine call. The victim mindset says, "I have no control; everything is happening to me," and it fosters a cycle of blame, helplessness, and self-doubt. Yet a man, called by God, is never destined to be a perpetual victim. Scripture declares that we are "more than conquerors" through Christ (Romans 8:37), revealing that our true posture is not one of defeat but of overcoming. Reclaiming a kingly mindset, therefore, requires shifting from self-pity and resentment to a stance of resilience, responsibility, and divine authority.

A victim mindset enslaves us because it absolves us of personal responsibility. If all blame can be laid at the feet of external circumstances—an unloving father, a hostile culture, or chronic adversity—then we never address how our responses might shape outcomes. We remain passive, waiting for others to fix our problems or wallowing in bitterness that keeps us trapped in emotional or spiritual stagnation. This posture also stunts spiritual growth because self-pity leaves little room for the boldness and creativity God wants to unleash in us. Furthermore, it corrodes relationships. Continual negativity turns people away, and promising opportunities fade when we lack the faith and initiative to pursue them.

The Bible refutes the notion that we are helpless. Throughout Scripture, God's chosen vessels have faced monumental setbacks—imprisonment, betrayal, exile. Yet these trials did not define them as victims; instead, their faith allowed them to transcend hardships. Joseph was sold into slavery by his brothers, framed for a crime he did not commit, and forgotten in prison. Yet he refused to see himself as a permanent casualty of others' cruelty. He leaned into God's presence and ultimately rose to save entire nations from famine (Genesis 37–50). His story underscores the power of adopting an overcomer's perspective: "What you meant for evil, God intended for good" (Genesis 50:20). Even adversity can become the breeding ground for greatness if we remain oriented toward God's redemption rather than lingering in self-pity.

Overcoming the victim mindset begins with accepting responsibility for our attitudes, choices, and the direction of our lives. Taking responsibility does not minimise the actual pain or injustice we have suffered. However, it does mean recognising that while we cannot always control what happens to us, we can control how we respond. Proverbs 24:10 warns against fainting in the day of adversity, suggesting that resilience springs from inward resolve rather than outward ease. A king under Christ's reign does not allow unfortunate events to dictate who he becomes; he invites the Holy Spirit to transform each trial into a stepping stone rather than a stumbling block.

A second dimension of moving from victimhood to victory involves reprogramming thought patterns. Negative self-talk—phrases like "I'll never succeed" or "I'm always unlucky"—can become self-fulfilling prophecies. Romans 12:2 commands us to "be transformed by the renewing of our mind," indicating that our internal narratives must align with God's promises rather than discouraging circumstances. Memorising verses that affirm your identity in Christ, such as Philippians 4:13 ("I can do all things through Christ who strengthens me") or 2 Timothy 1:7 ("For God has not given us a spirit of fear, but of power and love and a sound mind"), can systematically uproot defeatist mindsets. Over time, your inner voice transitions from "I'm a victim" to "I am more than a conqueror."

Community support also proves invaluable in shedding a victim mentality. Isolation fosters self-pity and blame-shifting, while fellowship with mature believers helps us see beyond our grievances. Confiding in trusted mentors or joining a men's group can challenge our distorted narratives about ourselves. Brothers in Christ can hold us accountable, urging us to see possibilities rather than dwelling on limitations. Sometimes, the very insight we need is a loving confrontation: "Brother, you're fixating on the negative; let's pray about a practical path forward." Such interventions remind us that God places people on our path to sharpen us (Proverbs 27:17) and push us toward His intended destiny.

Above all, the greatest catalyst for shifting from victim to overcomer is faith in God's sovereignty. Believing wholeheartedly that God can turn every challenge into a tool for transformation breaks the hold of self-pity. By resting in His ability to redeem even the darkest seasons, you no longer approach life as a powerless pawn. You learn to pray with expectancy, to step out in obedience rather than fear, and to interpret setbacks as teaching moments rather than final verdicts. You become more attuned to the Holy Spirit, seeking creative solutions where the victim mindset only sees dead ends.

Over time, adopting an overcomer's mindset reshapes every domain of your life—work, relationships, and ministry. You show up to challenges with readiness instead of reluctance, seizing opportunities to lead rather than complaining about obstacles. You speak hope into conflict-laden environments, defusing cynicism with the confidence of someone who knows God stands behind him. This posture also testifies to others that the gospel is not mere theory but a lived reality that enables us to transcend adversity. People drawn to your peace and resilience may eventually ask, "How do you remain hopeful?"—opening doors to sharing about the One who overcame the world (John 16:33).

Transforming your victim mindset does not mean denying your wounds or ignoring legitimate hardships; instead, it means choosing not to let them define your identity or destiny. God's grace is sufficient to convert your trials into triumphs, your scars into testimonies, and your grievances into stepping stones. You can take the next step confidently through divine strength, forging a path forward instead of circling in the wilderness of self-pity. In Christ, you are never destined for perpetual defeat. You were designed to govern your sphere of influence, reflecting God's reign by rising every time life knocks you down.

Thus, let adversity become your teacher, not your prison. Let each disappointment drive you deeper into faith, not drown you in complaint. Let each setback fuel your hunger for wisdom, not embitter you. As you reject victimhood, you reclaim your royal identity, the authority God has placed in you to make a difference in this world. This is the heart of true kingship: recognising that while hardships are inevitable, defeat is not. In every trial, an overcomer sees the seeds of a future victory, planted by a loving God who never wastes our pain but uses it to shape us into men worthy of the crown.

CLOSING THOUGHTS

Shifting from a victim to an overcomer mindset requires intentional steps: embracing personal responsibility, renewing your thoughts in alignment with God's promises, seeking a supportive community, and deeply trusting God's sovereign purpose through adversity. The victim mentality limits your growth and relationships, while adopting an overcomer's mindset empowers you to face life's challenges with resilience, courage, and faith. Like Joseph, your setbacks can become platforms for profound victories when viewed through the lens of divine redemption.

CALL TO ACTION

Now is the time to reclaim your kingly mindset. Identify the area of your life where you've allowed victimhood to hold you back. Commit to one practical step today: choose a scripture to memorise, reach out for accountability with a trusted mentor, or intentionally shift your inner dialogue to align with God's truth. Take ownership, step boldly into your divine calling, and become the overcomer you were created to be.

CHAPTER 7

IDENTITY IN CHRIST

A foundational truth of Scripture declares that those who belong to Jesus are not merely forgiven sinners but also "a chosen people, a royal priesthood" (1 Peter 2:9). These words are neither mere flattery nor a hollow metaphor; they identify the dual role to which every believer is called. On the one hand, you are royalty, entrusted with the authority to shape the spiritual and cultural climate around you for God's glory. Conversely, you function as a priest, bridging the gap between God and humanity through prayer, intercession, and the active demonstration of divine love.

Yet many men limit themselves to a single dimension, either focusing on spiritual pursuits without stepping into leadership or displaying confident leadership devoid of spiritual depth. True biblical manhood fuses both. By God's design, you have the right to boldly approach His throne of grace (Hebrews 4:16) and use that empowerment to lead effectively in the sphere He entrusted you.

Embracing this royalty first requires discarding the insidious lie that you are "just a nobody." When Moses encountered God at the burning bush (Exodus 3), he doubted his standing, worried he lacked the eloquence or authority to lead Israel to freedom. But God's response, "I AM has sent you," revealed that Moses would operate under divine sanction, not his frailties. The same holds true for you. Your perceived limitations do not override the fact that you are chosen and empowered by God. If you feel unremarkable—"just an average guy"—recognise that you are operating in Christ's authority, not your own.

Moreover, God's plan for your life does not rest on chance or your performance; it is rooted in His unwavering promise. Jeremiah 29:11 assures, "For I know the plans I have for you, plans to prosper you and not to harm you, plans to give you hope and a future." This prophecy, originally spoken to exiles facing an uncertain tomorrow, still reveals God's heart for all who trust Him. Even when your life's path seems unclear, you can stand on the promise that He has orchestrated a purpose suited explicitly to you. It is not enough to acknowledge you have a calling; you have to accept the invitation to step into your calling, believing He intends to prosper that calling, establishing it for His glory and for the flourishing of those around you.

A shift occurs when you truly accept this perspective. Suddenly, the mundane tasks that might seem unimportant—dropping your children off at school and tackling a routine job project—become arenas where God's grace can manifest. You carry an unseen crown that influences how you pray for your family, make ethical decisions at work, and interact with neighbours. Even the simplest routines can transform into Kingdom assignments if you see them through the eyes of a royal priest.

Scripture is filled with examples of ordinary people discovering they served an extraordinary God. Moses, reluctant and fearful, still stood up to Pharaoh. You may similarly be called to confront issues that seem more significant than your resources, yet because you wear the mantle of God's authority, you stand on a foundation more substantial than your doubts. And as Jeremiah 29:11 makes clear, you can remain confident that He intends these seemingly small steps to be woven into a bigger, hope-filled future.

Of course, the most accurate model of such authority is Jesus Himself. Thousands of voices try to define "real" manhood, from cultural icons to social media influencers, yet none captures true masculinity as Christ does. He is fully God yet humbled Himself, taking on human form (Philippians 2:6–8). He lived the example of unflinching authority—calming storms, casting out demons, confronting hypocrisy—and tender compassion, washing His disciples' feet (John 13) in a gesture typically assigned to the lowliest servant. There is nothing contradictory about bold leadership that stoops to serve; Jesus's life reveals that genuine kingship emerges when you wield power under God's guidance and harness it for others' benefit.

In stark contrast stands King Saul. He began with God's favour but allowed insecurity and impatience to rule his decisions (1 Samuel 13, 15). His jealousy of David exposed a man who coveted the throne without embodying the character required to lead righteously. Saul's downfall warns us that authority without grounding in godly humility degenerates into manipulation and control. Jesus's example, on the other hand, shows a better path. True kingship is rooted in divine calling and shaped by a willingness to serve, even when no one applauds. It protects rather than exploits, sacrifices rather than demands, heals rather than harms.

Yet, even if you accept this reality and attempt to model Jesus's humility and boldness, there is still a battlefield in your mind. Romans 12:2 admonishes you to be transformed by renewing your mind—systematically uprooting the self-defeating ideas, guilt, or shame that undermine your confidence. Lies like "I'll never measure up" or "I always fail" clash with biblical truths such as "I can do all things through Christ who strengthens me" (Philippians 4:13). This is not superficial optimism; it involves immersing yourself in Scripture until God's perspective becomes your instinctive outlook.

Elijah's burnout after his victory over the prophets of Baal (1 Kings 19) is a prime example. He had just witnessed God's miraculous intervention, yet a single threat from Jezebel sent him spiralling into self-pity and despair. God met him in that dark place, reminding him that he was far from alone and renewing his assignment. If Elijah, a towering prophet, could succumb to negative self-talk, how much more do we risk similar pitfalls? The antidote lies in exposing and correcting these mental scripts.

Such renewal is especially critical if you have been weighed down by past failures or sin. Though the chapter has spoken against "shame," it is vital to anchor this truth in the reality of being a new creation in Christ (2 Corinthians 5:17). At salvation, you are not simply improved or patched up; you are made brand-new. Your old record and identity are gone—God invites you to leave behind every regret that has shackled you. Embracing your identity in Christ includes fully releasing any condemnation or self-doubt rooted in what once was. It is a radical transformation that declares you are not defined by your worst mistake but by Christ's finished work.

A practical way to renew your mind is to memorise passages of Scripture that specifically counter your struggles—be they fear, anger, shame, or doubt. Take a few minutes daily to write down the negative loops echoing in your head, then challenge them with God's promises. Share your mind-renewal efforts with a friend or mentor who can keep you accountable. Over time, this deliberate reprogramming pushes back the territory the enemy has stolen in your thought life, enabling you to become the man God intended you to be. And in the process, you truly "walk in newness of life" (Romans 6:4), leaving old baggage behind (2 Corinthians 5:17).

Understanding your position in Christ means waking up daily knowing you are a royal priest—an ambassador of Heaven's authority and compassion. Like Moses, you might initially tremble at the enormity of the call, but "I AM" who empowers you remains sufficient to conquer every shortfall. Like Jesus, you can balance strength with service, never needing to dominate others to prove your worth. And, like Elijah, you can rest assured that when despair threatens to derail you, God's truth stands ready to realign your perspective and rekindle your purpose. Embracing your identity in Christ reshapes your spiritual life and how you engage in every aspect of existence. You stop travelling passively through the motions and begin to exert Kingdom influence on the people and projects under your care, confident that God has orchestrated a plan for you, as declared in Jeremiah 29:11.

Ultimately, your position in Christ is not about memorising titles like "royal priest" or "son of the King." It is about letting the reality behind those words transform your heart and habits. Confident in God's delegation of authority, you stand prepared to protect, build, serve, and bless in every sphere you occupy. You speak God's truth over your doubts and re-centre your mind with His promises. You look to Christ as the template for how to lead with humility. And you allow the Holy Spirit to chase away fear so you can move forward boldly in God's calling.

This is the glorious tension of living as both royalty and servant, leading with unshakable authority while stooping low to wash the feet of those around you. It is the life of a man who no longer sees himself as ordinary, but rather as a royal priest under the dominion of a King who calls him by name—fully trusting in God's future for him and living as a new creation, unburdened by any chains of the past.

One of the most powerful truths we can embrace is the finished work of the cross. Christ has accomplished everything necessary for our redemption, healing, and restoration. All the striving, labouring, and feeling of never being "good enough" dissolve when we understand that our Saviour's sacrifice has paid it all—once and for all. Our role, then, is to step into this victory by faith, allowing the transformative power of His grace to shape our lives. We don't have to earn His favour or His salvation; we accept, by faith, what He has already done. In this light, every worry, every burden, and every ounce of guilt can be left at the foot of the cross, where Jesus has already conquered them on our behalf.

CLOSING THOUGHTS

Understanding your identity in Christ transforms how you view yourself and your purpose. Scripture calls you a royal priest—chosen, empowered, and divinely appointed to influence the world around you through spiritual authority and servant leadership. Your true identity rejects limiting beliefs and past failures, resting firmly on God's promises and Christ's finished work on the cross. This powerful truth invites you into a life defined not by self-doubt or guilt but by the confidence and freedom in Christ. You are called to lead boldly, serve humbly, and renew your mind continually, allowing God's perspective to shape every aspect of your life.

CALL TO ACTION

Take practical steps today to embrace your royal priesthood. Identify negative beliefs that have held you back and confront each with the truth of Scripture. Begin memorising verses that directly counter your struggles and share your journey with a trusted friend or mentor who will hold you accountable. Let the reality of who you are in Christ shape your decisions, relationships, and actions, fully stepping into the calling God has uniquely designed for you. The victory Christ won on the cross is yours—live in it boldly.

CHAPTER 8

SPIRITUAL DISCIPLINE

A man who understands his kingship in Christ quickly realises that his authority will remain fragile without a robust spiritual foundation. The true strength in God's Kingdom is more than theoretical knowledge or one-time encounters; it is forged in the consistent application of spiritual disciplines. It is the daily act of prioritising God's presence, immersing oneself in Scripture, denying the flesh, and seeking accountability in a trusted community. Such practices are not optional add-ons; they are the scaffolding on which your faith—and ultimately your leadership—will stand or crumble.

Daily prayer serves as the unshakable foundation of your spiritual walk. Paul admonishes believers in 1 Thessalonians 5:16–18 to "pray without ceasing," urging an ongoing conversation with God. This instruction may sound daunting, but it fundamentally means placing yourself in a constant connection posture, letting God's presence inform your decisions, reactions, and emotions. Practically, it means setting aside intentional moments during your day to quiet your mind and engage in relational conversation with the Father, also expressing gratitude. Just as important is becoming still, allowing space for Him to share what is on His heart. Over time, these moments overflow into the rest of the day, weaving prayer into the very rhythm of life. Like a king conferring with the highest council, you seek God's perspective on daily choices. Rather than wandering, you walk confidently, guided by divine insight.

Yet prayer alone can become shallow if it lacks the anchor of Scripture. Joshua 1:8 proclaims that meditating on God's Word day and night leads to prosperity and success in the ventures God assigns. Scripture is not a mere historical record; it is a living, active truth that shapes how you see God and how you see yourself. When you consume the Bible regularly—reading, pondering, and listening for the Holy Spirit's application—it recalibrates your thoughts, sifting out cultural lies and self-deception. Your mind, once bombarded by societal pressures, begins to align with Kingdom principles. You find promises that speak to your daily situations, wisdom that keeps you from pitfalls, and a renewed sense of purpose that solidifies your kingship under Christ.

Fasting is another cornerstone practice often overlooked in modern church culture. In Matthew 6:16–18, Jesus assumes His followers will fast, not stating "if you fast" but "when you fast." Fasting humbles the flesh, intensifies spiritual hunger, and breaks strongholds that everyday routines cannot easily dismantle. It might take the form of skipping meals for a day, abstaining from certain foods, or even refraining from digital media to sharpen focus on the Lord. This discipline tangibly teaches dependence on

God, when your stomach growls, you learn to feast on divine sustenance instead of earthly comfort. Men who incorporate fasting regularly find their discernment heightened and their resolve fortified, as though the spiritual muscles are newly exercised and capable of greater endurance.

In the same way, consistent worship—both privately and corporately—nurtures faith from another angle. John 4:23–24 speaks of worshipers the Father seeks: those who worship in spirit and in truth. Singing songs of praise at home, participating wholeheartedly in congregational singing, and simply adoring God in silent reflection all work together to lift your eyes above life's immediate challenges. Worship reorients your heart, reminding you that you serve a King far greater than any earthly problem. In worship, your soul aligns with eternal reality, your anxieties yield to divine peace, and your kingship is grounded in the King of kings.

Even the fiercest warrior can fall if he lacks the right weaponry in battle. Jesus Himself demonstrated that Scripture memorisation is indispensable for combatting temptation. When tested by the devil in the wilderness (Matthew 4:1–11), Jesus did not argue or rationalise—He quoted written truth. "It is written," He declared, neutralising the enemy's ploys. If the Son of God utilised Scripture in spiritual warfare, how much more must we hide God's Word in our hearts? We reinforce our inner armoury by memorising passages—whether for resisting lust, battling discouragement, or seeking wisdom. When trials and deceptions strike, we respond with the clarity and power of God's promises rather than our fallible instincts.

Finally, no king remains strong in isolation. Accountability is vital for sustained growth. Proverbs 27:17 states, "As iron sharpens iron, so one man sharpens another." Even a man who prays, fasts, and studies Scripture can drift without brothers or mentors to challenge him. Relationships formed in mutual commitment to Christ foster transparency—environments where you can confess struggles, celebrate victories, and receive counsel. A king who refuses to isolate himself will benefit from others' strengths, insights, and prayers, weaving a spiritual safety net that catches him before he succumbs to temptation or despair. In this supportive fellowship, you stand less as a lone hero and more as part of a robust spiritual army.

Spiritual discipline is not about proving your holiness or ticking off religious tasks. It is about securing the foundation upon which your authority stands. Prayer keeps you in dialogue with the Ultimate Source of Wisdom. Immersion in Scripture curates your worldview toward Kingdom realities. Fasting breaks down the strongholds of carnal desire, redirecting your appetite to God. Worship breathes life into your faith, ensuring you do not lose sight of the greater narrative. Memorising verses outfits you with the spiritual sword to cut through lies, and brotherly accountability keeps you grounded in the shared pursuit of godliness. As you layer these disciplines into your life, you fortify your role as a king under Christ. No spiritual wind or wave can topple you when your roots go deep into God's presence and truth.

In a world that equates "real manhood" with impulsive bravado or passive neglect, spiritual discipline is a countercultural force. It builds an inner citadel from which godly leadership flows. These practices are not about instant gratification; they demand patience and steady perseverance. But for the man who invests in them, the rewards are exponential—deep intimacy with God, steady resilience in trials, a spirit unclouded by worldly noise, and a character that naturally commands respect. In short, you become the kind of king who leads not from insecurity or pride but from a heart so aligned with Heaven that it naturally blesses all those under your influence.

CLOSING THOUGHTS

A man's kingship under Christ is fortified by cultivating spiritual disciplines—daily prayer, Scripture immersion, intentional fasting, heartfelt worship, Scripture memorisation, and authentic accountability. These practices form the foundation for godly leadership, guarding against fragility and empowering steady resilience. Spiritual disciplines reorient your life toward divine wisdom, breaking strongholds, sharpening discernment, and connecting you deeply with God and others. This foundational strength transforms your leadership from insecure striving into confident influence grounded in eternal truth.

CALL TO ACTION

Do not settle for surface-level spirituality. Begin today to integrate these disciplines into your daily rhythm intentionally. Set aside dedicated times for prayer, immerse yourself consistently in Scripture, engage in heartfelt worship, memorise the Word, align yourself with His truth, and seek genuine accountability. Take the next step now—choose one discipline you have neglected or overlooked and purposefully incorporate it into your week. Your kingship in Christ is waiting; step boldly into the disciplined life God has called you to live.

CHAPTER 9

POWER OF A KING'S WORDS

A king's words have the ability to shape not only his destiny but also the atmosphere around him. In Scripture, we see that life and death lie in the power of the tongue (Proverbs 18:21). God created all things by speaking them into existence, and we, made in His image, mirror that same creative potential whenever we open our mouths. Yet, just as words can build and heal, they can also tear down and wound if wielded carelessly. True kingship demands a disciplined tongue, one that consistently reflects the character and authority of the King of kings.

A king who speaks casually or rashly forfeits much of his influence. His words, meant to call forth greatness, become a source of confusion or even harm. Consider the biblical accounts of kings whose decrees altered the course of entire nations. Their success or failure often hinged on the integrity and wisdom behind what they declared. Today, you may not sign official edicts or royal proclamations, but your everyday speech still sets the spiritual and emotional tone for those around you—your family, coworkers, friends, and community. Every word you speak either moves them closer to God's purposes or distracts them from it.

One hallmark of a godly king's speech is that it builds rather than breaks. Ephesians 4:29 reminds believers to speak only words that edify and impart grace to the listener. This principle applies doubly to men with Kingdom authority. When you talk to your spouse, your children, your colleagues, or those you mentor, do your words instil courage and direction, or do they bring discouragement and confusion? As the apostle Paul counsels, your speech should be a wellspring of life, inspiring faith in God's promises. Even in correction, a king's words guide rather than condemn, aiming for restoration rather than punishment.

The power of a king's speech also hinges on consistency between word and action—a man who promises more than he delivers and flatters but never follows through erodes trust. When Jesus taught, people marvelled at His authority because His life backed up His words. He spoke from a purity of heart that left no contradiction between what He said and who He was. Similarly, as a man seeking to manifest God's Kingdom, you must let your "yes" be yes and your "no" be no (Matthew 5:37). If you say you will show up, show up. If you say you will pray for someone, actually pray. If you speak about generosity, demonstrate it in tangible ways. Hypocrisy crumbles a man's authority; consistency cements it.

Sometimes, you will need to speak words of confrontation or warning. Love and truth go hand in hand. James 3 illustrates the influential nature of the tongue, comparing it to a rudder guiding a massive ship. If you see a loved one drifting into danger, your role as a king under Christ compels you to speak, not out of anger or self-righteousness, but of genuine concern for their well-being. This correction, spoken in humility, can steer someone away from destruction. On the other hand, silence can be as destructive as reckless words, for it withholds the truth that could save a life or reclaim a destiny.

At the same time, a king's speech calls forth greatness. As God spoke life into Adam, you can speak life into those around you, affirming their worth in Christ and reminding them of the destiny God has carved out for them. Simple statements like "I believe in you," "God has equipped you," or "Your gifts are essential in our community" can unlock hearts that have closed off under years of criticism or neglect. Too many men offer criticism freely but withhold praise, leaving those in their care starved for any sense of accomplishment. In contrast, a kingly approach is to name the gold in others—to see beyond flaws or mistakes and declare the potential God placed within them.

Remember also that your words shape your mindset. What you speak over yourself matters immensely. If you constantly declare defeat—"I can't handle this," "I'm never going to change"—you align your heart with negativity rather than with the power of God. Jesus stated that the mouth speaks from the abundance of the heart (Luke 6:45). If your heart meditates on faith, Scripture, and God's promises, your mouth will reflect that. Over time, you become what you consistently speak because your words direct your focus, prayers, and actions.

At the core of your kingship lies the truth that you were created in the image of God—the God who formed reality with His voice. He spoke, and worlds were shaped. Light burst forth. Life began. Your reality is continually being shaped by your words, which hold both spiritual and practical weight. With your mouth, you influence the atmosphere around you, the condition of your heart, and the future you are walking toward. What you consistently speak, you begin to believe. What you believe, you begin to live. And what you live ultimately forms the reality you experience.

Words are not just sounds—they are seeds. Every time you speak, you plant something—in your marriage, in your children, in your workplace, and in your soul. You create an environment of faith, hope, and strength or fear, doubt, and defeat. That's why a king watches his tongue. He doesn't just speak his feelings; he speaks his future. He speaks life into dead places. He calls things forth as though they were. His words are not random—they are intentional tools that align with the Spirit of God.

To speak carelessly is to surrender your authority. To speak wisely is to partner with Heaven in shaping your destiny. A king understands that the power of life and death is in the tongue—not just metaphorically, but tangibly. His reality is forged first in the spirit, then manifested in the natural. So, he speaks with vision, discipline, and conviction—because he knows what comes out of his mouth is already shaping what lies ahead.

Finally, you must stay tethered to God's Word to guard your mouth effectively. Immerse yourself in Scripture so your thoughts and language naturally reflect biblical truth. Surround yourself with brothers in Christ who will challenge you when your words become harsh or self-seeking. Practice quieting your soul before you speak, asking the Holy Spirit to guide your responses in tense situations. Over time, these small disciplines shape you into a man whose words hold healing, wisdom, and divine authority.

A king's greatest arsenal is not just in his deeds but in his declarations. When you speak life and truth consistently, you cultivate an atmosphere of faith and expectation. You break strongholds of doubt and fear by announcing God's perspective, not man's. You foster unity where division threatens to grow and hope where despair lingers. In short, your speech becomes an extension of God's Kingdom reign, inviting others to step into the reality of His grace and power. That is the weight and the privilege of speaking like a king who serves under the greatest King of all.

CLOSING THOUGHTS

Your words hold immense spiritual power. As a man reflecting the authority of Christ, your speech can either build and heal or tear down and wound. True kingship means consistently aligning your words with God's truth, demonstrating integrity by matching speech with action, and courageously speaking life into others and yourself. Your words shape your atmosphere, influence your community, and determine your future and legacy.

CALL TO ACTION

Today, take a moment to evaluate your words. Identify one area—your family, workplace, or personal declarations—where your speech can better reflect God's truth and purpose. Commit to intentionally speaking life, hope, and affirmation in that area. Ask the Holy Spirit to guide your tongue, and watch how your words begin to transform your world.

CHAPTER 10

STANDING IN AUTHORITY, WALKING IN HUMILITY

Bold leadership and genuine humility may seem at odds, but Scripture reveals they can coexist powerfully in a man who understands his position in God. The world often equates boldness with arrogance or domineering behaviour. Yet, the Bible describes a different kind of confidence—a boldness that flourishes because it rests on humble dependence on the Lord. Far from frailty or passivity, meekness is directed strength placed under God's authority, ready to move decisively yet constantly aware of who grants the power.

Joshua embodies this delicate balance. When Moses died, Joshua was commissioned to lead the Israelites into the Promised Land, an exhilarating and daunting task. Repeatedly, God urged him to be "strong and courageous" (Joshua 1), but Joshua never interpreted this as a license to dominate or act recklessly. He chose instead to seek God's guidance before each major undertaking, demonstrating that real courage springs from continual reliance on divine wisdom. Boldness and humility propelled Israel to epic victories. By contrast, men who rely solely on personal skill or brute force often collapse under the weight of pride and the absence of spiritual grounding.

Just as Joshua's humility shaped his leadership style, so must we address any shame or hidden sin that undermines our confidence. Conviction from the Holy Spirit nudges us to repent and evolve, but shame whispers that we are unworthy—that certain failings or addictions disqualify us from rightful authority. When guilt lingers, it corrodes faith and paralyses our capacity to lead. In John 4, Jesus encounters a Samaritan woman who suffers profound shame after a series of failed relationships. Rather than condemn her, He offers "living water," effectively restoring her sense of worth and commissioning her to spread the good news. That moment of grace shattered her belief that she was too tainted to matter.

Men often hold onto regrets that feel similarly disqualifying. It may be a moral collapse, a shattered marriage, or a betrayed friendship. Yet the Bible overflows with redemption stories: David was called a man after God's heart despite his adultery. Paul transitioned from persecutor of believers to apostle of grace. Peter, who denied Jesus three times, rose to become a pillar of the early Church. Each found that sincere repentance opens the door to renewed confidence, allowing them to stand in God's authority without fear of condemnation. When you accept Christ's atonement, you lose the right to shame yourself further. You learn to walk, no longer weighted by sins He has already forgiven.

This spiritual freedom lays the groundwork for practical authority in everyday life. A man standing in God's strength—yet aware of his ongoing need for grace—will lead with firmness and compassion. Such leadership entails active steps. First, it means initiating prayer in your household or sphere of influence, not waiting passively for others to do so. Gathering your spouse or children for prayer before meals, bedtime, or whenever challenges arise sends a clear message that you trust God's power above your own. It also involves safeguarding your personal and familial "kingdom." You identify and remove detrimental influences: toxic relationships, harmful online temptations, or unhealthy habits that can erode your moral footing. Beyond guarding, a king must show initiative.

Nehemiah exemplifies this readiness to act. On learning that Jerusalem's walls lay in ruins (Nehemiah 1–2), he prayed fervently, then approached his earthly king for resources to rebuild. Undeterred by ridicule, threats, or the enormity of the project, he combined humility in seeking God's guidance with a decisive labour organisation. His readiness to defend the city, inspire the workers, and confront external opposition reveals a man living out authority without lapsing into tyranny. This mixture of bold leadership and godly submission culminates in restored walls and renewed hope for his people.

Perhaps the key lies in rejecting the false dichotomy that equates authority with pride. True biblical authority is stewarded with a servant's heart, just as Jesus—fully God—knelt to wash His disciples' feet. It is prepared to say, "I must decrease so that He may increase," yet not shrink from courageous action when God's name or your entrusted responsibilities are at stake. Such a posture befits men who have reconciled with their past, whether moral failures or hidden shame, and who now walk steadily under His forgiveness. They speak life into others, champion their families, lead prayer in small circles or large gatherings, and persist with calm tenacity even when challenges loom.

In the end, standing in authority means you understand your rightful place as a son of the King, entrusted to protect and guide those within your domain. Walking in humility means you never forget who grants you that power and that you remain forever reliant on His Spirit. This fusion of confidence and lowliness produces a stable environment for everyone around you, mirroring the life of Christ Himself—a life marked by unstoppable purpose yet underscored by a willingness to serve. If you embrace that balance, you guard your soul and the hearts and destinies of those who depend on your leadership.

CLOSING THOUGHTS

Bold leadership and genuine humility are not contradictions but divine companions. True authority in God's Kingdom arises from humble dependence on Him, empowering you to lead decisively without pride. Joshua and Nehemiah model how humility combined with courageous faith leads to victory and restoration, while Jesus Himself illustrates perfect authority expressed through servant-hearted humility. By addressing hidden shame, repenting sincerely, and embracing God's forgiveness, you become a confident yet humble leader, equipped to powerfully influence your family, workplace, and community.

CALL TO ACTION

Today, make a deliberate choice to walk confidently in the authority God has entrusted to you while continually surrendering your pride and self-reliance. Take immediate action: initiate prayer within your family, address and remove harmful influences from your life. Embrace this biblical balance—stand firm in God's authority and walk humbly in His grace.

CHAPTER 11

DECISION-MAKING

Each day presents many minor and routine decisions, others weighty enough to alter your future. As a king under Christ's authority, your choices shape your life and the well-being of your family, community, or anyone under your influence. More than mere logic or convenience, kingly decision-making entails seeking divine wisdom, weighing potential outcomes, and honouring God's will. When you view decisions through this lens, you steward your authority responsibly, fostering growth and stability in the realm entrusted to you.

Central to this approach is understanding stewardship. First Corinthians 4:2 underscores that faithful stewardship of all God has placed under your care—finances, relationships, talents, and time—marks the heart of biblical kingship. You pause before acting impulsively, remembering that your choices affect long-term legacy. Joseph's story in Genesis 41 is a striking example: given oversight during seven years of plenty in Egypt, he carefully devised a resource plan that saved nations during subsequent famine. True kingship asks you to consider, "How will this decision affect those under my care?" A mindset fixed on the good of those you lead prevents self-serving or impulsive actions.

Scripture provides multiple models of wise decision-making. In 1 Kings 3, God offered Solomon anything he desired, and Solomon chose to ask for wisdom to govern effectively. Such humility pleased God, who responded by granting both riches and honour. Solomon's priority was the Kingdom's well-being rather than personal gain, reminding us that decisions shaped by service often lead to broader blessings. In contrast, 1 Kings 12 shows Rehoboam rejecting the counsel of wise elders, following harsher peer advice, and ultimately splitting a once-united nation. His example warns that the voices we heed can strengthen or destroy our leadership. Nehemiah (Nehemiah 1–2) blends prayer with strategy, crying out to God about Jerusalem's broken walls and securing resources from his earthly king to rebuild. He balanced spiritual dependence and organised planning, exemplifying that faith and practical steps go hand in hand.

Adhering to these biblical patterns compels you to seek God first. Matthew 6:33 exhorts you to pursue His Kingdom and righteousness above all else. Praying and immersing yourself in Scripture beforehand safeguards you from hasty influences or fleeting emotions. It also emphasises the need for godly counsel. Proverbs 11:14 teaches that a multitude of wise advisers fosters stability and success. Rather than making choices in isolation, you consult mentors, pastors, and spiritually mature friends who can expose blind spots. Once you gather insight, you project both short- and long-term consequences. Asking how a path might affect your family's future or spiritual growth months or years later, and ward off rash or short-sighted decisions.

In addition to wise counsel, the Holy Spirit's inner prompts are valuable guides. Often, you'll sense a nagging unease or a profound peace around a particular option. Don't ignore these nudges. Pause, pray, and delve deeper. Scripture, wise mentors, and the Spirit's guidance frequently align, confirming your course. Even after all this discernment, bold faith remains essential. Making a momentous decision can spark resistance or fear—like Joshua facing the Promised Land with its imposing giants (Joshua 1:9). Courage is not the absence of fear but a willingness to trust God and move forward anyway. It's in such faith-driven leaps that your kingship is tested and refined.

Ultimately, each decision becomes another stroke on the canvas of your life and legacy. God has entrusted you with the authority to lead and the responsibility to ensure your leadership echoes His heart. Challenges will inevitably appear, and uncertainties will persist, yet your posture should remain one of reverence and obedience to the One who called you. Over time, consistent, God-honouring decisions forge credibility in your household and community. They unify your family behind a clear moral compass and offer a deep sense of fulfilment, knowing you have stewarded your authority for God's glory. Reflect on Joshua's unwavering courage, Solomon's prayer for wisdom, Nehemiah's deliberate planning, and Joseph's stewarded foresight. When you integrate their lessons—seeking God, valuing wise counsel, honouring biblical principles, and stepping out in courageous faith—you develop the lifestyle of a king who governs his life, home, and broader circle with wisdom and grace. As you remain faithful in these daily judgments, you paint a lasting portrait of trust, unity, and significance, leaving an imprint that resonates far beyond your lifetime.

CLOSING THOUGHTS

This chapter shows that kingly decisions should never be made casually under Christ's authority. Instead, they require divine guidance, careful consideration of consequences, and a willingness to act courageously—always keeping the well-being of others in mind. By following the examples of biblical leaders like Joseph, Solomon, Nehemiah, and Joshua, you learn how prayer, wise counsel, practical strategy, and bold faith can shape decisions that honour God and inspire those you lead.

CALL TO ACTION

Before making your next critical decision—big or small—pause and seek God first. Pray, consult Scripture, and invite mature, godly counsel. Ask yourself how your choice will affect the people entrusted to your care. Then, take action boldly, trusting God's leading. Such purposeful, faith-filled decision-making will allow you to rule your life and sphere of influence with true wisdom and grace.

CHAPTER 12

KINGDOM FINANCES

One of the most significant paradigm shifts in a man's journey to kingship is the raw, humbling realisation that he owns nothing—everything belongs to God. The money in your account, the home you inhabit, the business you guide, and the skills you harness for income are not yours. You are not an owner but a steward. This truth should upend your entire approach to finances. Recognising that every resource in your care serves a divine purpose frees you from chasing wealth for security or status. Instead, money becomes a powerful tool to honour God, provide for your family, and bless others. In embracing this revelation, you enter a realm of limitless resources—no longer bound by earthly economies.

This doesn't mean financial success is unimportant. Scripture does not condemn wealth but warns against the love of money (1 Timothy 6:10). The issue isn't possessing resources but how you manage and prioritise them. Kingdom-minded financial stewardship is about working diligently, saving wisely, investing responsibly, giving generously, and refusing to allow greed, fear, or debt to enslave you. It's about aligning your financial decisions with God's will rather than with societal pressures or fleeting material desires.

Psalm 24:1 reminds us, "The earth is the Lord's, and everything in it." This truth dismantles the illusion of self-made success and forces you to view your financial life through the lens of stewardship. The biblical story of Joseph highlights this principle. He was placed in charge of Potiphar's house (Genesis 39) and later over the resources of Egypt (Genesis 41). He did not own the wealth he managed, but God positioned him to influence nations because he was a faithful steward. Joseph's wisdom in storing grain during years of plenty ensured survival during famine. His story exemplifies the principle that when you manage resources well, you set yourself—and others—up for stability, impact, and blessing.

Jesus reinforced this mindset in the Parable of the Talents (Matthew 25:14–30). The master gave different sums of money to three servants, expecting them to invest and multiply it. The first two doubled their portion and were rewarded. The third, ruled by fear, buried his talent and was rebuked. This parable underscores a powerful lesson: God expects you to use and grow what He gives you. Faithful stewardship means holding onto what you have and maximising its impact. Avoiding financial responsibility—whether through poor planning, excessive risk-taking, or failing to give—is a failure of stewardship.

A crucial element of Kingdom finances is generosity. Second Corinthians 9:6–7 teaches that "whoever sows sparingly will also reap sparingly, and whoever sows generously will also reap generously." Giving is not just a transaction but an act of worship and trust. Many people struggle with generosity because they fear lack. But when you give, you acknowledge that God is your provider. Generosity disrupts greed, shifts your heart from possessions to people, and opens doors for God's provision in ways beyond human logic. He doesn't need your money—He is after your heart. And your heart is often tied to your finances. To see where your priorities lie, examine where your cash flows.

Paul warns against the dangers of an unhealthy attachment to wealth in 1 Timothy 6:6–10. He emphasises that contentment, not accumulation, is the key to peace. Many men are constantly pursuing more, convinced that their financial security depends on an ever-expanding bank balance. But contentment frees you from the anxiety of always striving for what's next. It allows you to enjoy and use money wisely without letting it define your identity or purpose. A king does not hoard wealth for its own sake; he deploys it for maximum impact—in his family and in the Kingdom of God.

Practical financial stewardship starts with budgeting and planning. Jesus said, "Which of you, wishing to build a tower, does not first sit down and count the cost?" (Luke 14:28). A man who does not plan his finances is setting himself up for unnecessary stress and potential ruin. Having a financial roadmap ensures that your resources align with Kingdom priorities. If your money is constantly running out before the month does, or if you're spending aimlessly, it's time to get organised. Know where your money is going, allocate funds for giving and saving, and avoid spending on fleeting indulgences with no eternal value.

Tithing is not about giving God something that belongs to us but returning a portion of what already belongs to Him. Everything we have is His, and tithing is a tangible act of acknowledging His provision and lordship over our finances. Malachi 3:10 calls us to bring the whole tithe into the storehouse, not as a burdensome obligation, but as a demonstration of faith and obedience. While some debate the specifics of tithing under the new covenant, the principle of intentional, regular generosity remains. It is not a religious requirement to check off a list; instead, it is a discipline that cultivates trust in God rather than in wealth. When you tithe, you sow a seed that aligns your heart with God's priorities, ensuring that money never becomes an idol. But giving must always be done with the right motives—not to manipulate God into blessing you but as an act of surrender and faith. He searches the heart, and giving flows from a place of gratitude and trust, not control.

Saving and investing wisely are also biblical principles. Joseph saved grain in Egypt, ensuring a future crisis did not lead to disaster. Proverbs 21:20 teaches that "the wise store up choice food and olive oil, but fools gulp theirs down." Wise men prepare for the unexpected. This might mean having an emergency fund, making sound investment choices, or avoiding reckless financial decisions. However, the danger comes when saving turns into hoarding—when you trust your reserves more than you trust God. Stewardship requires balance: saving diligently but also remaining open-handed in generosity.

Debt is one of the greatest financial traps that enslaves men today. Proverbs 22:7 warns that "the borrower is a slave to the lender." While some debt, like a mortgage or business investment, can be strategic, most consumer debt is a burden that weighs men down and hinders financial freedom. Excessive debt creates stress, damages relationships, and limits your ability to give. If debt is already a struggle, commit to eliminating it. Ask God for wisdom and provision to break free from financial bondage so that you can move into greater Kingdom stewardship.

Accountability in financial matters is essential. Many men suffer in silence with financial burdens because they are too ashamed to seek help. But Scripture emphasises the wisdom of counsel. Proverbs 11:14 reminds us that "where there is no guidance, a people fall, but in an abundance of counsellors there is safety." Whether it's seeking guidance from a mentor or trusted friend, involving wise counsel in your financial decisions can prevent costly mistakes and keep you grounded in biblical principles.

If you want to shift into a Kingdom financial mindset, take inventory. Look at your assets not as personal trophies but as Kingdom tools. If you don't have a budget, create one this week. If you already have a financial plan, review it through the lens of stewardship—where can you increase giving, where can you cut excess, and how can you realign your money with eternal priorities? Find someone to hold you accountable, whether it's a friend, spouse, or mentor, and commit to financial transparency.

Finally, dedicate your finances to God in prayer. Lay your income, debts, savings, and spending before Him, declaring, "Lord, these belong to You. Guide me to manage it with wisdom, integrity, and generosity." When you surrender your resources, you step into the freedom of stewardship, releasing the anxiety and pressures of financial control and embracing the peace of divine provision.

Embracing the reality that you own nothing and steward everything transforms your financial life. It liberates you from the exhausting chase of material gain and aligns you with God's heart of generosity, wisdom, and faithfulness. A king under Christ's rule does not live anxiously, constantly striving for more—he operates with trust, knowing that his provision is secured in the hands of a sovereign God. In a world obsessed with wealth accumulation, you stand as a beacon of something greater: a man who manages finances with integrity, gives with a joyful heart and trusts in the One who provides all things.

CLOSING THOUGHTS

Recognising that everything we have belongs to God completely reframes how we handle money. Instead of chasing wealth for status or security, we become faithful stewards who manage resources with wisdom, generosity, and humility. By viewing finances through this Kingdom lens, we break free from fear and greed and instead use money to honour God, provide for our families, and bless others. This mindset isn't about neglecting financial success; it's about ensuring that every decision—from tithing and saving to investing and giving—flows from a heart aligned with God's will.

CALL TO ACTION

Take a practical step toward faithful stewardship. Draft or review your budget, identifying where you can be more intentional with giving, saving, and spending. Invite accountability—ask a friend, mentor, or spouse to walk alongside you and offer wise counsel. Finally, dedicate your finances to God in prayer, declaring, "Lord, these belong to You. Guide me to manage it with wisdom, integrity, and generosity." In doing so, you move closer to living as the kingly steward God has called you to be.

CHAPTER 13

HONOURING THE TEMPLE

A king does not neglect his kingdom or the temple he has been given—his own body. How a man treats his physical being reflects his discipline, self-respect, and awareness of the divine purpose placed within him. This is not vanity; it is stewardship. A man's body is not his own—it is a temple entrusted to him by God, meant to serve as a vessel of strength, vitality, and endurance. When a king allows his body to fall into neglect—through poor nutrition, laziness, or lack of self-care—he limits his ability to lead, protect, and fulfil his calling with excellence.

A neglected body is a vulnerable body. Weakness, fatigue, and preventable illnesses creep in when a man dismisses the importance of what he puts into himself. Food is not just for pleasure—it is fuel, and like a warrior preparing for battle, what a man consumes determines his energy, mental sharpness, and ability to function at his highest capacity. A king does not run his kingdom on scraps or fuel his body on processed, artificial substances that slowly wear him down. He eats with wisdom, knowing that food feeds his strength or destruction.

There is no room for gluttony in a man who seeks to walk in dominion. Overindulgence—whether in sugar, fast food, or excessive portions—enslaves the body and dulls the spirit. A king practices discipline not because he is obsessed with his appearance but because he refuses to be mastered by anything. He eats to build, sustain, and sharpen his body for the mission ahead. He sees his meals as investments in longevity, not just fleeting moments of gratification. He drinks water, not sugar-laced sodas that offer nothing but sluggishness. He chooses real nourishment over artificial substitutes because he understands that what he consumes will prepare him for battle or weaken him before the fight begins.

A king moves his body. He does not live in perpetual stillness, allowing himself to grow sluggish, immobile, and undisciplined. His body is meant for action, for strength, for endurance. He does not idolise exercise or turn his physique into an object of worship, but he trains his body with diligence, staying capable, strong, and ready. He understands that movement is a gift; every stretch, every run, every lift is more than just about building muscle—it's an act of stewardship. It is about maintaining the ability to stand firm in his purpose. A weak body cannot support a strong calling. A man constantly fatigued, out of breath, or weighed down by his own neglect cannot be fully present for his family, work, or mission. A king trains because he honours what has been given to him. He builds stamina, cultivates endurance, and refuses to let his body deteriorate through apathy.

Yet, physical strength alone does not define a king. A man's presence—how he carries himself and presents himself to the world—speaks volumes before he ever utters a word. A king does not walk in public with his pants sagging and his clothes wrinkled, with an image that communicates carelessness and disorder. He does not dress for vanity, but he does dress with honour. He understands that his appearance is a reflection of his mindset. He does not need luxury brands or extravagant clothing, but he ensures that his clothes are clean, fitted, and appropriate for the man he is called to be. A king does not step out looking like a boy without direction. He carries himself with dignity and an upright posture, his attire reflecting the discipline he upholds in every other area of his life.

There is a level of self-respect in a man who keeps himself well-groomed and whose presence commands respect without arrogance. He does not dress to seek validation from others; rather, he recognises that how he presents himself reflects his values. He wears clothes that fit him well and reflect his role as a leader and a man of purpose. He does not allow himself to be sloppy because sloppiness in appearance often bleeds into sloppiness in thought and action.

A king understands that caring for his temple is not about ego but readiness. He does not allow laziness, gluttony, or neglect to rob him of the strength, the confidence, or the energy he needs to fulfil his calling. He eats to fuel, moves to strengthen, and dresses to reflect the order he carries within him. He does not abuse his body, nor does he worship it. He honours it. He stewards it. He treats it as a tool entrusted to him, meant to be sharpened, refined, and used for a greater purpose. And in doing so, he stands as a man who is fully prepared—spiritually, mentally, and physically—to walk in the full authority of his kingship.

Jesus treated His body as a sacred trust. He grew strong in Joseph's workshop and on Galilee's dusty roads, rising early to pray yet stepping away to rest when needed. He savoured simple meals by the fire but also embraced seasons of fasting, proving that discipline and delight can coexist. His example invites us to steward our bodies with the same balanced devotion.

CLOSING THOUGHTS

A king's body is not merely his own—it is a sacred temple entrusted to him for a higher purpose. Maintaining health and fitness is not an act of vanity but one of stewardship, discipline, and respect. By fuelling himself with proper nourishment, exercising diligently, and presenting himself with dignity, a man positions his body and spirit for strength and readiness. His physical habits echo his inner values and directly impact his ability to lead, protect, and fulfil his calling with excellence.

CALL TO ACTION

Take a moment to assess your daily habits. Commit to fuelling your body with clean, nourishing food, moving regularly to build endurance, and dressing in a way that reflects your identity and purpose. Decide today that you will not allow neglect or apathy to rob you of the vitality and clarity you need to fulfil your divine mandate. Honour your temple, embrace discipline, and walk out your kingship with excellence.

CHAPTER 14

WHOLESOME HOBBIES AND ENTERTAINMENT

A king does not fill his life with empty things. He understands that how he spends his free time shapes the strength of his mind, the health of his heart, and the direction of his spirit. In a culture saturated with passive entertainment and constant distraction, it is easy to become numb, feeding on amusement that leaves the soul undernourished. But a man of kingship lives with intention. Even his leisure reflects his identity and values.

Hobbies are not indulgences; they are investments. They either fuel growth or drain purpose. A wholesome hobby builds rather than breaks, strengthens rather than weakens. It may restore creativity, sharpen discipline, cultivate rest, or forge connections. Whether it is woodworking, reading, gardening, music, sports, or adventure—every hobby is an opportunity to reflect the image of God, who created, cultivated, and delighted in His creation.

What you do when no one is watching often reveals what you value most. Are you wasting hours scrolling through social media, binge-watching shows that degrade your spirit or losing time to mindless entertainment that stirs comparison, envy, or lust? Or are you engaging in things that enrich your mind, bring joy to your soul, and prepare your heart for the calling God has placed upon your life?

Even the purest hobby becomes a threat when it costs you your kingdom. If your entertainment causes your wife to feel alone, your children to feel unseen, or your home to feel neglected, then what once gave life is now quietly stealing it. A king who disappears into his pleasures while his family withers in silence isn't resting—he's retreating.

Leisure should refresh you, not replace your responsibility. No game, no screen, no pursuit is worth more than your presence at the table of your legacy. A man who escapes into entertainment while his household starves for connection is not harmless—he is dangerously absent. The enemy doesn't always destroy with violence. Sometimes, he subtly distracts, numbing the heart until the crown slips.

A true king knows how to rest but never forgets what he's been entrusted to protect. Enjoyment is a gift, but never let it cost you your marriage, fatherhood, or spiritual leadership. Guard what God has given you. And never trade your throne for a momentary escape. The king guards the gates of his soul. He filters what enters through his eyes, ears, and imagination. Not everything permissible is beneficial (1 Corinthians 10:23). A wise man does not allow amusement to become an anaesthetic. Entertainment should refresh, not enslave. Ask yourself: does what I watch, play, or listen to draw me closer to Christ or subtly desensitise me to sin?

There is beauty in rest and recreation. Jesus Himself withdrew to quiet places, not to escape, but to recharge and refocus. Rest is holy when it is purposeful. Hobbies can be a sacred rhythm that prevents burnout and realigns your soul. They can bond you to your children, connect you with your spouse, or place you on the path of men who need your influence.

Wholesome entertainment doesn't mean living a boring life. It means living a life rooted in greater joy. It means having fun without guilt, engaging your passions without compromise, and laughing freely without losing your moral compass. True kings don't need vulgarity to find humour, nor darkness to feel depth. They know that joy is not found in cheap thrills but in the richness of a life anchored in truth.

So, evaluate your habits. What hobbies do you need to revive? Which ones do you need to release? What kind of man are your hobbies shaping you to become? A king doesn't waste his time. He builds. He restores. He creates. He plays with purpose. And when he rests, he does so with peace, knowing even his entertainment glorifies the King of kings. Reclaim your time. Redeem your joy. And let your hobbies reflect the man you are becoming.

CLOSING THOUGHTS

In a world that glorifies busyness and numbs with distraction, the king stands apart—not because he rejects rest, but because he redeems it. His leisure is not careless but intentional. He understands that how he spends his time when no one is watching reveals the man he truly is. How he rests, plays, and enjoys life is not random—it reflects his values, priorities, and calling. Hobbies are not an escape from life; they are part of the life he is building. They can refresh the soul or rot the foundation, depending on how they are held. The king does not apologise for enjoying life, but does not excuse indulgence that costs him his crown. His joy is clean. His fun is guilt-free. And his rest is sacred—not because it's religious, but because it's aligned with purpose. This is the mark of a man who knows that even in his downtime, he is still guarding a kingdom.

CALL TO ACTION

Take inventory of your time. Look honestly at the hobbies, habits, and entertainment that fill your days—do they build or break you? This week, choose one area where you've been passive or indulgent and realign it with purpose. Maybe it's deleting an app, setting boundaries around screen time, or reigniting a hobby that brings life and connection. Ask yourself daily: *Is this shaping me into the man, I'm called to be?* Don't just consume—create. Don't just escape—engage. Set a standard for your free time that honours your values and reflects your kingship. Start now. Reclaim your time, restore your focus, and lead—even in how you rest.

CHAPTER 15

DATING LIKE A KING

In a culture where dating has become a casual pursuit, many men enter relationships with little thought about their purpose or impact. The world teaches that dating is about personal gratification, moving from one relationship to another without much reflection. It encourages men to avoid commitment, test their options, and prioritise pleasure over responsibility. But as a man of God, your relationships should reflect your identity in Christ. Dating is not a game—it is preparation for covenant. How you approach relationships now is shaping the foundation of your future marriage. Your choices today will not disappear once you say, "I do." They will strengthen or weaken the bond you will one day share with your wife.

Dating like a king means taking full responsibility for the relationship's direction, clarity, and integrity from the beginning. In God's divine design, man initiates, leads, and sets the tone for what's to come. From the start, Adam was given identity, purpose, and responsibility before Eve was brought to him—not so she could pursue him, but so she could be received, cherished, and protected. A king does not play with emotions, avoid clarity, or keep his options open; he honours the woman before him by being intentional, honest, and direct. A woman should never be left wondering where she stands, whether she is wanted, or carrying the emotional weight of defining the relationship. If she finds herself initiating, leading, or trying to pull commitment out of a man, it is a clear sign that something is out of alignment. That burden was never hers to bear. A man who is not willing to pursue is not ready to lead. Pursuit is not about chasing—it's about covering. It reflects Christ's leadership toward His bride: protective, intentional, and rooted in love. Masculine leadership begins with pursuit, and anything less distorts godly order. If you are serious about a relationship, you will say so. You will not waste her time. You will not shrink back. A king rises, leads with integrity, and pursues with purpose.

Dating like a king requires intentionality. It is not about seeing how much you can get from a woman, but how well you can protect, honour, and lead her. When you understand that dating is a pathway to marriage, you become mindful of your actions, words, and decisions. You do not engage in relationships to fill a void or satisfy a temporary craving for companionship. Instead, you date with the mindset of building something that will last. A man of God does not enter a relationship recklessly—he approaches it with wisdom, maturity, and a commitment to doing things God's way.

Your ability to lead in dating directly reflects your ability to lead in marriage. If you date without accountability, discipline, or self-control, those same tendencies will carry over into your role as a husband. Leadership in a relationship is not about control but creating an environment where love, trust, and honour can flourish. How you treat a woman in dating sets the precedent for how you will treat her as your wife. If you are careless, inconsistent, or selfish now, marriage will not suddenly transform you into a man of integrity. Growth begins in singleness.

A relationship should never be built on emotional highs or fleeting attraction. While chemistry and connection are important, they are not the foundation of a lasting bond. The ultimate question is: Are you spiritually and emotionally prepared to lead a woman in a way that reflects Christ's love for the Church? Leadership in dating means more than just making plans or deciding where to go on a date. It means taking responsibility for the relationship's purity, direction, and purpose. It means recognising that the woman you pursue is a daughter of God and should be treated with respect.

Sexual purity is one of the most significant marks of leadership in a man. It is not simply about avoiding physical sin—it is about training yourself to master your desires rather than being mastered by them. Purity is a mindset, a discipline, and a commitment to honouring God and the woman you are with. The world sees purity as unnecessary and outdated, but a man who values purity understands its purpose. He knows that self-control before marriage is a reflection of faithfulness within marriage. When a man cannot restrain himself in singleness, he will struggle with restraint when challenges arise in his marriage.

Pursuing purity is not just about avoiding temptation but about developing a heart that seeks righteousness in all things. It is about guarding not just your actions but your thoughts, your words, and your intentions. A relationship built on purity fosters trust, respect, and emotional security. It removes guilt, shame, and confusion and replaces them with clarity, peace, and a deeper connection. It shows a woman that her worth is not tied to what she can offer physically but to who she is in Christ. Purity is not about deprivation—it is about preservation. It is about reserving the fullness of intimacy for the covenant of marriage, where it can be embraced and cherished without fear, regret, or consequence.

Leadership in dating is displayed through consistency. A stable man in his emotions, decisions, and faith creates a safe space for a woman to trust and be vulnerable. He does not disappear when things get complicated. He does not send mixed signals or manipulate through silence. He does not make empty promises. He follows through with his words and is unwavering in his pursuit. His consistency is a testament to his character, proving that he is not ruled by feelings but by conviction.

The story of Boaz and Ruth offers a glimpse into what honourable pursuit looks like. Ruth, a widowed foreigner, found herself in a vulnerable position. Many men would have taken advantage of her circumstances, but Boaz did the opposite. He covered her with protection, treated her with dignity, and provided for her needs. He did not see her as a temporary distraction but as a woman of great worth. He did not rush the process or demand anything from her—he honoured her by ensuring she was safe and provided for. Boaz pursued Ruth with integrity, patience, and respect, showing that a man's true strength is displayed in how well he protects, not how much he takes.

A king does not wait for marriage to become a leader—he begins leading in singleness. He builds the habits, disciplines, and mindset to carry into his future relationship. He will not magically become a responsible husband overnight if he is passive, indecisive, or careless before marriage. He prepares himself spiritually, emotionally, and mentally so that when he enters a relationship, he can offer something meaningful rather than rely on a woman to complete him.

The greatest gift a man can give his future wife is a heart that God has already tested, refined, and strengthened. A man who has developed discipline in his thoughts, actions, and relationships will step into marriage equipped to love selflessly, lead wisely, and remain faithful under any circumstance. His relationship with God is his foundation, and from that foundation, he learns how to love, honour, and pursue a woman in a way that reflects Christ's love for the Church.

Dating as a king is not about meeting cultural expectations but living according to Kingdom principles. It is about rejecting society's standards of temporary pleasure and choosing the higher calling of self-control, responsibility, and honour. It is about valuing commitment over convenience and integrity over indulgence. A man who dates like a king is not swayed by the world's definition of masculinity—he defines manhood by the way he protects, leads, and pursues.

A king builds for legacy, not for momentary pleasure. He does not waste time on relationships that do not align with his purpose. He does not chase distractions. He focuses on what matters, knowing that every decision he makes today shapes the life he will live tomorrow. The man who chooses to date with honour, purity, and intention is not just preparing for marriage—he is preparing to be the kind of husband, father, and leader God has called him to be. That is dating like a king.

CLOSING THOUGHTS

Dating like a king is about intentionality, honour, and foresight. It is choosing to protect and esteem the woman you pursue rather than seeking what you can gain from her. A man of God recognises that dating is marriage preparation—a sacred opportunity to develop the character, discipline, and selflessness that a covenant demands. By prioritising purity, clarity, and consistency, you lay the groundwork for a relationship that reflects Christ's love for the Church. Your leadership in singleness foreshadows the kind of husband you will become, and every decision you make now shapes the legacy you will leave tomorrow.

CALL TO ACTION

Determine today that you will not settle for casual, aimless dating. Reflect on the habits and mindsets you need to refine and actively seek accountability. Set clear boundaries, communicate your intentions, and commit to protecting and honouring the woman you are with. Above all, cultivate a deeper relationship with God—allow Him to shape your heart and motives so you can lead with integrity and courage. Dating as a king starts now.

CHAPTER 16

SEXUAL PURITY

Sex is one of the most powerful forces in a man's life. It can build or destroy, heal or wound, strengthen or corrupt. The world treats sex like a recreational activity, something to be indulged in without consequence. But the truth is, sex was never meant to be casual. God designed it as a sacred bond, a fire that warms and unites when contained within the marriage covenant but consumes and destroys when unleashed without restraint. A man who does not master his sexual desires before marriage will struggle to control them in marriage. Purity is not a switch that flips on the wedding night; it is a discipline forged in the secret battles of singleness and upheld in the daily marriage choices.

A king rules over his appetites—they do not rule him. The world says that abstinence is unrealistic and that a man cannot be expected to control himself. But the very essence of masculinity is self-discipline. A man who cannot control his urges is not strong—he is weak. He is enslaved by his desires, a servant to his own passions. The true strength is in mastery, in the ability to say no to temptation, to resist the momentary pleasure that leads to long-term regret. Sexual purity before marriage is not just about waiting—it is about training. It is about proving that you can be trusted with a woman's heart and body because you have first learned to honour God with your own.

Many men think that marriage will solve their struggle with lust. They believe that once they have a wife, their sexual desires will be contained and fulfilled. But marriage does not cure lust—it only exposes what was already there. A man who indulges in pornography, casual sex, or unrestrained desire before marriage will bring those same habits into his covenant. If he could not control himself before, he will not magically gain self-control after. Lust is never satisfied. It always demands more. The only way to master it is to kill it before it kills you.

Moreover, many men fall into the trap of believing masturbation is harmless simply because Scripture does not address it by name. Yet the principles are clear: Jesus equates lust in the heart with adultery (Matthew 5:28), and masturbation typically fuels lust by centring on self-gratification rather than self-control. It can feed isolation, guilt, and a distorted view of sexuality that prioritises instant relief over a covenant-based bond. First Corinthians 6:18 urges believers to "flee from sexual immorality," not to accommodate it. What seems like a private act can condition a man to seek pleasure without the sacrificial love, discipline, and unity that real intimacy requires. Over time, this self-centred pattern undermines purity in both singleness and marriage, dulling sensitivity to the Spirit and eroding the character needed to cherish a spouse. A king's strength lies in learning to master his desires, not in granting them unchecked permission.

Sexual purity before marriage is not just about avoiding physical sin. It is about preparing for faithfulness in every area of life. A man who disciplines his eyes, mind, and body before marriage is not restricting himself; he is strengthening himself. Purity is not deprivation but preparation. It ensures that when you enter marriage, you carry no baggage of past mistakes, no comparisons, no hidden struggles—only a heart wholly committed to one woman. Purity is a gift to your future wife, proof that you honoured her long before you even met her. But purity is not just about the past—it shapes the future.

The habits you form in singleness determine the faithfulness you will walk in during marriage. Staying true to your wife is not just about physical loyalty; it is about guarding your heart, protecting your covenant, and ensuring your love remains pure and undivided. The greatest weapon against temptation is not willpower, but a heart surrendered to God. A man who walks closely with Christ finds that purity is not a burden but freedom. It is the ability to love fully, without distraction, regret, and compromise. A king chooses purity not because he has to but because he knows that a divided heart can never build an unshakable kingdom.

For men who have already stumbled, the grace of God offers restoration. Purity is not just about where you've been. It's about where you choose to go from here. A man who repents and resets his standards can walk in freedom, no longer chained to past mistakes. God does not require perfection, but He does require pursuit. The pursuit of holiness, righteousness, and a life that honours Him in every aspect, including sexuality.

Sexual purity does not end at the altar. Many men think that once they are married, the battle is over. But the truth is, purity within marriage is just as important as purity before it. The enemy knows that if he can corrupt a man's view of intimacy, he can fracture the foundation of his home. Infidelity does not begin with an affair—it starts with unchecked thoughts, subtle compromises, and emotional disconnection that allows temptation to take root. A married man must be just as vigilant in guarding his mind, eyes, and affections as before marriage.

Pornography is one of the greatest silent killers of marriages today. It creates unrealistic expectations, distorts true intimacy, and breeds dissatisfaction. A man who entertains lust in his heart while married is already stepping outside of his covenant, even if his body has not followed. Jesus made it clear in Matthew 5:28: *"Anyone who looks at a woman lustfully has already committed adultery with her in his heart."* The standard for purity is not just in actions but in thoughts, intentions, and secret moments when no one is watching.

A king does not betray his queen in action, thought, or hidden desires. He fights for the purity of his marriage with the same intensity that he fought for his singleness. He does not allow unchecked fantasies to create distance between him and his wife.

He does not open doors to temptation by entertaining conversations, images, or desires that do not belong within his covenant. He understands marital intimacy is physical, emotional, spiritual, and sacred. He does not take his wife for granted or seek fulfilment outside the love God has given him.

A man who is faithful in marriage is not just avoiding adultery—he is actively pursuing his wife. He intentionally keeps their connection alive, ensuring that his affections are fully invested in her. He speaks life over her, cherishes her, and makes her feel desired, not just for her body but for her heart, mind, and soul. He understands that intimacy is not just something that happens in the bedroom—it begins in how he speaks to her, honours her, and leads her spiritually.

The world laughs at purity. It mocks self-restraint. But the world also suffers from broken marriages, addiction, betrayal, and the emptiness that comes from chasing pleasure without purpose. A man who chooses purity chooses strength. A man who honours his body before marriage and his wife after marriage chooses a path of stability, fulfilment, and a lasting legacy.

A king does not live by his impulses. He does not trade his destiny for a moment of indulgence. He sees the bigger picture. He understands that purity is not about restriction—it is about freedom. Freedom from guilt, from regret, from addiction. Freedom to love one woman fully and be present in his marriage without divided affections. Freedom to stand before God and know that he has honoured Him in one of the most sacred areas of life.

Sexual purity is not a burden—it is a weapon. It guards your soul, protects your marriage, and strengthens your leadership ability. The man who masters his desires before marriage will be trusted to steward intimacy well within it. The man who walks in purity does not just build a strong marriage—he builds a legacy of faithfulness that will outlive him, setting a standard for future generations. That is the power of a king who chooses purity.

CLOSING THOUGHTS

God designed sex as a powerful, sacred bond meant to unite spouses in a covenant of trust. When treated casually, however, it can quickly consume and destroy. Purity is not simply avoiding physical sin—it's a lifelong discipline that shapes your ability to love well and honour God. A man who masters his desires before marriage prepares himself to cherish his wife with undivided commitment afterwards. Even within marriage, ongoing vigilance is essential since unchecked thoughts can erode intimacy and open the door to greater temptations. The true strength is surrendering to God, allowing Him to transform lust into genuine love, and choosing faithfulness as a daily act of leadership and devotion.

CALL TO ACTION

Don't settle for a culture of compromise—choose to be the king who masters his appetites and builds a life free from regret. Begin by bringing your hidden battles into the light—confess them to God and share them with a trusted mentor. Then, commit to practical steps that guard your heart and renew your mind. Let purity define your approach to intimacy, whether single or married. Refuse to be ruled by momentary desires; instead, stand firm in the freedom and strength from honouring God with your body, thoughts, and deepest affections.

CHAPTER 17

KING, PRIEST & HEAD OF THE HOME

A man who steps into marriage enters more than a relationship—he steps into a divine calling. He is no longer just a man; he becomes the head of a household entrusted by God with his wife's spiritual, emotional, and physical well-being. This headship is not about control—it is about responsibility. It is about dying to self, leading with humility, and loving with unwavering commitment. Ephesians 5:25 sets the standard: "Husbands, love your wives, just as Christ loved the church and gave Himself up for her." Christ loved when it was hard. He loved through betrayal, rejection, and silence. That is the measure of a king's love in marriage.

God's divine order in marriage is not about power plays or rigid hierarchy—it is about harmony, protection, and purpose. When a man embraces his God-given role as head of the home, he is not claiming superiority but stepping into divine accountability. Just as Christ is the head of the Church and gave Himself for her, the husband is called to lay down his life for his wife, not once, but daily. This sacred order reflects Heaven's architecture: Christ over the man, the man over his household, each role flowing not in competition but in unity. When a husband leads in love, and a wife responds with trust, a divine current is released—one that brings peace, favour, and supernatural covering into the home.

The enemy knows the weight of this design. He understands that the entire body suffers if he can strike the head. He doesn't need to destroy a family—he only needs to dethrone the king. If he can twist a man's leadership into control or render it passive and disengaged, the atmosphere of the home breaks down. That's why the war against men is so aggressive—because a man walking in his rightful authority under Christ is a direct threat to the enemy's agenda. When a husband leads with courage, humility, and the sacrificial love of Christ, his marriage becomes a fortress, his wife flourishes, his children thrive, and his legacy becomes one that hell cannot shake.

A weak man believes leadership is dominance—making demands, controlling every decision, expecting submission without question. But a king understands that true authority earns trust, not fear. A man who leads well does not need to assert his power; it is evident in how he speaks, serves, and sacrifices. His wife does not follow him out of fear but from great honour because she knows he follows Christ first.

Adam's failure in the Garden was not just that he sinned—it was that he stayed silent. He watched as the serpent deceived his wife and said nothing. He failed in his responsibility to protect. And many men today repeat Adam's mistake. They retreat into silence, distraction, or apathy and leave their wives unprotected—

emotionally, spiritually, and relationally. They grow passive, blaming their wives for the distance, failing to see that their absence—of presence, pursuit, and prayer—is the true root of the disconnect. A king does not abandon his post. He steps up. He leads. He intercedes. He protects what God has entrusted to him.

Marriage is a covenant, not a contract. A contract depends on performance, but a covenant is anchored in commitment. Love is not a fleeting emotion but a deliberate choice, a sacred vow reaffirmed daily. A husband's words build or destroy the climate of his home. Harshness, criticism, and neglect drain the atmosphere of intimacy, while tenderness, honour, and vision breathe life into it.

Selfishness is a silent assassin in marriages. A man who expects his wife to serve him while he disengages is not a leader—he's a burden. A king serves beside his queen. He pursues her heart, not just her body. He listens, protects, and creates emotional safety. He ensures his wife knows she is seen, heard, and cherished. A man who neglects his wife yet demands respect is like a farmer who refuses to water the soil but expects a harvest.

Kingly leadership is marked by consistency. A husband who prays over his wife leads spiritually and initiates resolution instead of prolonging the conflict, builds a home that weathers any storm. He does not watch his wife carry emotional and spiritual burdens alone—he carries them with her. He repents when he falls short, seeks forgiveness when he wounds, and guards the unity of the home with diligence. He does not see leading as ruling over—he sees it as lifting up.

The legacy of a king is not carved in accolades or assets—it's etched in the hearts of those closest to him. It is in the peace his wife sleeps in. It is in the confidence his children walk in. It is in the strength of a marriage that has weathered the storm and stood firm. A man who loves well does more than lead a marriage—he anchors generations in righteousness.

Your wife is not a supporting character in your story. She is your queen, your greatest gift, your sacred assignment. You are called to love her with fierce intentionality. To protect her not only from harm but from neglect. To honour her, not only in public, but in private. Because one day, you will not stand before God to give account for how impressive you were to the world—but for how faithfully you loved the woman He entrusted to your care.

God's order isn't there to limit—it's there to bless. When it's honoured, marriages flourish. When it's abandoned, everything suffers. Rise, King. Your throne is not for control—it's for covering. Reign with sacrifice. Lead with humility. And love with the strength of Christ Himself.

CLOSING THOUGHTS

A husband's divine calling is to lead his marriage with responsibility, humility, and sacrificial love. He is to guard against passivity, serve his wife wholeheartedly, and build a secure environment that nurtures intimacy and mutual respect. Authentic leadership is not demanding or domineering; humble actions, loving words, and the consistent pursuit of unity mark it. A man who embraces this calling reflects Christ's love, leaves a legacy, and honours the God-given covenant of marriage.

CALL TO ACTION

Consider your leadership honestly: Where have you pulled back instead of stepping forward in love? Commit today to one practical step that strengthens your marriage—initiate prayer together, speak words of affirmation, or admit when you're wrong and seek forgiveness. Make a daily choice to prioritise your wife's well-being, protect her heart, and lead with honour. Active love and dedicated leadership can transform your home and leave a powerful legacy.

CHAPTER 18

FATHERHOOD IS YOUR LEGACY

Fatherhood is more than a biological role—it is a divine calling. Whether raising biological children or mentoring spiritual sons, your influence as a father shapes the next generation in ways beyond your lifetime. Psalm 127:3–5 declares that "children are a heritage from the Lord," a blessing entrusted to a man's care. But fatherhood is not just about providing for their physical needs; it is about shaping their identity, faith, and understanding of what it means to be loved. It is one of the highest responsibilities a man can carry, and how you lead in this role will determine whether you leave behind a legacy of strength or brokenness.

The foundation of fatherhood is presence. You cannot lead from a distance. Many men assume that as long as they provide financially, their duty as fathers is fulfilled. But children do not just need food and shelter—they need you. They need face-to-face moments, undivided attention, and genuine connection. They need to know that their father is emotionally available, not just physically present in the house. Many wounds in men today trace back to fathers who were absent—not necessarily because they abandoned their families, but because they were too preoccupied, too emotionally closed off, or too passive to engage deeply. Your presence in your child's life is a greater gift than anything money can buy.

A godly father speaks life over his children. In Matthew 3:17, God the Father declares over Jesus, "This is My beloved Son, in whom I am well pleased." Before Jesus performed a single miracle, before He accomplished anything in His ministry, He was affirmed by His Father. This moment reveals a powerful truth—sons (and daughters) need to hear their father's voice speaking love and affirmation over them. Your words shape your child's self-worth and identity. If you fail to affirm them, the world will step in with its destructive messages. A father's blessing creates confidence; his silence creates insecurity. It is not enough to assume your child knows you love them—tell them. Say, "I'm proud of you," "I love you," and "You have what it takes." These words, spoken consistently, can change a child's life trajectory.

A father's role also includes discipline, but discipline must be rooted in love, not anger. Correction without connection leads to rebellion. Children need guidance, but they also need grace. Ephesians 6:4 warns fathers, "Do not provoke your children to anger, but bring them up in the discipline and instruction of the Lord." This means that discipline should never crush a child's spirit or make them feel unloved. Too many fathers swing to extremes—either being too harsh and controlling or too passive and disengaged. But a godly father knows how to balance discipline with warmth. He sets boundaries but also provides reassurance. He corrects but also forgives. And when he makes a mistake, he is humble enough to apologise. There is no greater lesson in leadership than showing your child what true repentance looks like.

One of the greatest failures in fatherhood is neglecting to address sin and moral drift in the home. The story of Eli, the priest, serves as a sobering warning. Eli's sons were corrupt, abusing their priestly positions by exploiting the people and dishonouring God (1 Samuel 2–3). Eli knew about their wickedness but failed to correct them effectively. He offered weak rebukes but took no decisive action. Eventually, God held him accountable, and his family suffered severe consequences. This highlights an important truth: as a father, you are responsible for your household's moral and spiritual direction. Do not look the other way if you notice your children straying into destructive behaviour. Lovingly confront, set firm boundaries, and guide them back to God's ways. Passive fatherhood creates space for disorder and dysfunction. True fatherhood requires courage—the willingness to address sin, not out of control, but out of love.

Beyond parenting, fatherhood extends into mentorship. Many young men today grow up without strong male role models. They navigate life without guidance, making costly mistakes that could have been avoided if someone had stepped in to lead them. If God has positioned you as a mentor, take that role seriously. A spiritual father is not just someone who gives advice; he walks alongside, invests time, and helps shape another man's future. Paul modelled this relationship with Timothy, referring to him as "my true son in the faith" (1 Timothy 1:2). If you do not have biological children, that does not exempt you from the responsibility of fatherhood. There is always a younger man who needs your wisdom, encouragement, and example.

Your legacy as a father is not determined by wealth, achievements, or status—it is determined by the impact you leave on those who come after you. If you fail as a father, nothing else will compensate for that loss. If you succeed, your influence will echo through generations. The question is, what kind of legacy are you building? Will your children and spiritual sons remember you as a man who led with love, wisdom, and strength? Or will they remember a man who was distant, passive, or harsh? The choice is yours.

Fatherhood is a reflection of God's nature. As His sons, we are called to model His love, discipline, and grace. He is both just and merciful, both strong and compassionate. Intimacy with God is crucial to raising children and equipping them with Heaven's call on their lives. Whether you are raising children in your home or mentoring young men in your community, you are shaping destinies. Do not take this calling lightly. Step into it fully, knowing that the way you lead today will define the men of tomorrow.

CLOSING THOUGHTS

Fatherhood is a profound calling that extends beyond mere provision. It is about being genuinely present—emotionally engaged and attentive to your children's or spiritual sons' needs. A godly father not only affirms, instructs, and disciplines with love but also sets a lasting example through consistent character, humility, and courage. Whether you have biological children or mentor others, your words and actions form the bedrock of a legacy that shapes future generations.

CALL TO ACTION

Choose today to be intentional about fatherhood. Make time to connect deeply, speak words of life, and lead by example in both discipline and grace. Seek out opportunities to mentor younger men who lack a strong role model. Remember, fatherhood is not a role you fulfil—it's a legacy you build. Embrace it wholeheartedly and watch how God uses your influence to transform lives and impact the next generation.

CHAPTER 19

RESOLVING CONFLICT

Conflict is inevitable. Whether in marriage, fatherhood, friendships, or the workplace, disagreements will arise. But as a king under Christ's authority, how you handle these conflicts determines the strength of your leadership, the stability of your home, and the legacy you leave behind. Many men either avoid confrontation or engage in it aggressively, but neither approach brings true resolution. Biblical conflict resolution aims not to win an argument but to strengthen relationships, foster unity, and grow in wisdom. When approached correctly, every conflict becomes an opportunity for deeper understanding, greater connection, and spiritual refinement.

One of the first things a king must recognise is that conflict is not merely about the issue at hand—it often exposes deeper heart issues. James 4:1 asks, "What causes fights and quarrels among you?" The answer points inward: unspoken fears, unmet expectations, and unresolved wounds fuel most arguments. A disagreement about finances may stem from a man's fear of inadequacy as a provider. A conflict with a child over discipline might reveal an internal struggle with patience or authority. How you react to conflict says more about your heart than the situation itself. Instead of seeing conflict as a problem, view it as a mirror—an opportunity to see where God calls you to grow, mature, and refine your leadership.

Cain and Abel's story in Genesis 4 serves as a warning. Cain's anger toward Abel wasn't really about his brother—it was about his own insecurity and his unmet desire for God's approval. Instead of addressing his internal struggle, Cain let bitterness consume him, leading to tragic consequences. The lesson is clear: unaddressed wounds in a man's heart can manifest as destructive conflict. But when a king recognises these underlying issues, he can address them with wisdom and grace, preventing division and fostering reconciliation.

A wise king does not allow conflict to escalate unchecked. Jesus said, "Blessed are the peacemakers, for they will be called children of God" (Matthew 5:9). Being a peacemaker is not about avoiding difficult conversations or allowing toxic behaviour to continue. It is about standing in the gap as Jonathan did for David when King Saul sought to harm him (1 Samuel 19). Jonathan risked his safety to bring peace, demonstrating that true conflict resolution requires courage and humility. It means listening to all sides, seeking truth, and acting with integrity rather than impulse.

As a leader in your home, you set the tone for how conflict is handled. If you respond with anger, blame, or withdrawal, you teach those around you to do the same. But if you respond with patience, wisdom, and a commitment to resolution, you model a Christ-like approach to reconciliation. The first step in handling conflict is to slow down. James 1:19 instructs, "Be quick to listen, slow to speak, and slow to become angry." Too often, men rush to defend themselves, formulate their rebuttal before fully hearing the other person, or react emotionally instead of responding thoughtfully. A wise king pauses, listens, and seeks to understand before speaking.

One of the most powerful conflict resolution tools is how you communicate. Instead of pointing fingers and making accusations, shift your language to reflect vulnerability and ownership. Saying, "You never listen to me," creates defensiveness, while saying, "I feel unheard when..." fosters open dialogue. Making your experiences and feelings known allows for honest conversations without triggering unnecessary resistance. Holding back in conversations hinders restoration; true healing comes when everything is brought to light.

A sincere apology is often the bridge to reconciliation. Many men struggle with admitting fault, believing it makes them appear weak. But the true strength is in humility. A man who can genuinely say, "I was wrong, and I'm sorry," gains the respect of his family rather than losing it. A king does not let pride stand in the way of peace. Instead, he initiates healing conversations, even when he is not solely to blame. This sets the example for those under his leadership, teaching them that taking responsibility is a mark of true manhood.

It is also essential to identify the real issue beneath the surface. Many arguments are not about what they seem on the surface. A husband and wife may fight over how household chores are divided, but the deeper issue may be a feeling of imbalance or unappreciation. A father and son may argue about curfews, but the real conflict may be about trust and independence. Instead of arguing about surface-level complaints, ask, "What is the deeper issue we need to address?" When the genuine concern is uncovered, it can be dealt with effectively rather than being buried under repeated petty arguments.

One of men's most significant mistakes in conflict is prioritising winning over restoration. Ephesians 4:26 warns, "Do not let the sun go down while you are still angry, and do not give the devil a foothold." Holding onto resentment or fighting to prove a point can create lasting damage in relationships. A king understands that true leadership means choosing unity over personal victory. It means conceding when necessary, apologising when needed, and always prioritising the relationship.

Healthy conflict resolution also requires follow-up. After the emotions settle, revisit the conversation. Ask, "How do you feel after our discussion? Is there anything still unresolved?" This ensures that conflicts are not just temporarily set aside but genuinely resolved. A king does not allow wounds to fester—he ensures they are fully healed so they do not resurface later.

To create a healthy communication culture in your home, consider implementing structured time for open dialogue. A weekly family meeting allows everyone to share their concerns, victories, and struggles in a safe space, reducing the chances of unspoken frustrations building into larger conflicts. Additionally, for married couples, a weekly covenant meeting—a 30-minute conversation to discuss the logistics of the home, responsibilities, and areas where support is needed—can prevent misunderstandings and strengthen unity.

Conflict, when handled correctly, does not destroy—it builds. It deepens trust, strengthens relationships, and refines character. As a servant-king, you are called to lead with wisdom, humility, and a commitment to reconciliation. Instead of avoiding hard conversations or reacting with anger, choose to navigate disagreements with patience, honesty, and a focus on restoration. A home that embraces healthy conflict resolution becomes a fortress of peace, where love is stronger than offence, and grace is greater than pride.

At the heart of every conflict is a choice: Will you allow it to divide, or will you use it as an opportunity to grow? Jesus Himself is the ultimate peacemaker, reconciling us to God despite our rebellion. When you follow His example, you turn moments of tension into stepping stones of growth, forging deeper bonds and leaving behind a legacy of wisdom, strength, and grace for future generations.

CLOSING THOUGHTS

Conflict is not the enemy; unaddressed heart issues are. Rather than avoiding or dominating disagreements, a Christ-centred king seeks to listen, understand, and resolve them. By pausing before reacting, communicating honestly and humbly, and prioritising restoration over "winning," you foster a home where unity and growth flourish. In this way, conflict becomes an opportunity to draw closer to those you love and to deepen your character, ultimately strengthening the legacy you leave behind.

CALL TO ACTION

Examine your own heart the next time conflict arises. Ask God to reveal hidden fears, pride, or insecurities that fuel the tension. Then, lead boldly by initiating humble dialogue, owning your part, and seeking genuine reconciliation. Make peace-making a hallmark of your leadership, and watch as your home becomes a refuge of unity, trust, and grace.

CHAPTER 20

THE REFINER'S FIRE

No matter how strong, every king will face trials that shake the foundation of his rule. Life's challenges do not indicate failure; they are the fire through which true kings are forged. The world tells men to avoid pain, to numb themselves, or to blame others for their struggles. But a king does not shrink back. He faces hardship with a different mindset—one that refuses to waste suffering, knowing that challenges are not meant to destroy him but to refine him into the man God has called him to be.

A king does not get to choose the battles that come his way, but he does get to choose how he responds. Hardship can either forge him into an unshakable leader or break him into a passive victim. His willingness to embrace pain as part of his training is the difference. Just as gold is purified through fire, a man's character is refined in the furnace of affliction. Trials expose what is hidden, revealing weaknesses, refining strengths, and stripping away false confidence so that his dependence is placed firmly on God.

When trials come, it is tempting to resist them, to wish them away, or to ask, *Why me?* But resistance to pain only prolongs the lesson. There are seasons when God allows a man to go through hardship, not because He has abandoned him, but because He is preparing him for greater responsibility. Consider Joseph, betrayed by his brothers, falsely accused, and imprisoned. If Joseph had not endured the suffering of betrayal and false imprisonment, he would never have been positioned to govern Egypt and save an entire nation from famine. His trials were not a detour but the road to his destiny.

Pain is a teacher that demands attention. If ignored, it repeats the same lesson in different forms until it is learned. A man who does not confront his pain will find himself facing the same struggles over and over, circling the same mountains of insecurity, anger, or fear. But a king who embraces the lesson hidden in the hardship will emerge stronger, wiser, and more prepared for the battles ahead. He will graduate instead of repeating the test.

Suffering has a way of stripping away pretence. When a man is in the fire, his true heart is revealed. Does he turn to God or worldly distractions? Does he lash out at others or allow humility to do its work? Trials expose the heart's motives and bring to light areas that require transformation. They are not meant to weaken a king but to strengthen him. The fire does not destroy gold—it purifies it.

The enemy wants nothing more than for a man to be crushed under the weight of his struggles. He whispers lies amid hardship:

You are alone. You are failing. You will never get through this. But the truth is, a king never faces his battles alone. God stands in the fire with him, just as He did with Shadrach, Meshach, and Abednego. They were thrown into the furnace, but they were not burned. Why? Because the fourth man in the fire was Christ Himself. The presence of the King is what sustains a man in the flames.

Victory does not come from escaping trials but from enduring them with faith. A man who stands firm in suffering becomes a leader who cannot be shaken. He does not let challenges define him; he lets them refine him. And in that refining, he gains the wisdom and strength to lead his family, community, and himself with authority and grace.

If you are facing hardship, do not run from it. Do not numb yourself or grow bitter. Instead, ask, *What is God trying to teach me through this?* Let pain do its work. Allow it to strengthen your dependence on God, humble your heart, and forge your character. You will come out of the fire, but you will not come out the same. You will emerge refined, tested, and ready for the battles ahead.

A king is not measured by how easy his life is, but by how he endures when everything around him is tested. The storms will come, but the man who stands on the Rock will remain unshaken. This is the path of a true king—one who does not waste his trials but lets them sharpen him into a vessel of power, wisdom, and unbreakable faith.

CLOSING THOUGHTS

Hardships are not meant to destroy you; they are the fires that refine you into the man God has called you to be. By embracing trials instead of running from them, you allow pain to expose weaknesses and strengthen your character. In the furnace of adversity, you discover the power of depending on God, shedding false confidence, and emerging with unshakeable faith. Like gold purified by fire, you will not be consumed but transformed.

CALL TO ACTION

Do not waste your trials. Face the fire head-on, asking God what He wants to reveal and refine in you. Resist the urge to numb your pain or blame others, and instead, let adversity strengthen your faith, sharpen your focus, and deepen your dependence on the One who stands with you in every battle. As you endure, you will rise as a king who leads with wisdom, authority, and a tested unbreakable resolve.

CHAPTER 21

ACCOUNTABILITY AND GROWTH

A king who stops growing stops leading. The moment a man believes he has arrived, he begins to decline. Stagnation is the silent killer of kingship, luring men into complacency with past victories and blinding them to the battles still ahead. True kingship is not a title but a relentless pursuit—of wisdom, refinement, and alignment with God. No man drifts into greatness. It is fought for, cultivated, and sustained with discipline and intention.

Many men experience spiritual highs—perhaps after a powerful sermon, a weekend retreat, or a deep conversation that stirs the soul—only to return to old patterns within weeks. Why? Because they mistake inspiration for transformation. Emotion may ignite a fire, but only discipline keeps it burning. A king does not rely on fleeting motivation; he builds a foundation of habits that keep him rooted when emotions fade. He does not let his guard down, knowing that the enemy does not attack when he is most alert but when he is most comfortable.

Scripture warns of the dangers of complacency. *"Let anyone who thinks he stands to take heed lest he falls"* (1 Corinthians

10:12). The greatest defeats do not come during the war but in the ease that follows victory. King Hezekiah trusted God for miraculous deliverance, yet later, in a moment of pride, he displayed his kingdom's wealth to foreign envoys. That seemingly harmless act led to the downfall of future generations. The lesson is clear: past obedience does not guarantee future faithfulness. A king must remain vigilant. What he fails to protect today, his children will have to fight for tomorrow.

A wise king surrounds himself with men who sharpen him. *"As iron sharpens iron, so one man sharpens another"* (Proverbs 27:17). A man left to himself will justify his weaknesses, excuse his sins, and drift into mediocrity. Accountability is not optional—it is the safeguard against self-deception. True accountability is not a casual check-in but an open door to challenge, correction, and truth. It is the willingness to be confronted and refined, even when it is uncomfortable. The men who avoid accountability are the same men who fall when the weight of leadership becomes too heavy to bear alone.

Growth is not a seasonal effort; it is a lifelong commitment. A man who was strong in his twenties but unwise in his fifties did not lose his wisdom overnight—he simply stopped pursuing it. Joseph moved through multiple seasons: a favoured son, a betrayed slave, a forgotten prisoner, and ultimately, a ruler of nations. At every stage, he had to adapt, learn, and seek God's wisdom for what lay ahead. He would never have been ready for the throne if he had remained bitter in prison. Likewise, a man cannot afford to get stuck in the identity of a past season. Each phase of life requires a new depth of wisdom, a deeper surrender, and a greater willingness to grow.

Spiritual intimacy is the fuel that sustains a man through every transition. Without it, even the strongest men crumble. A king who neglects his time with God is like a warrior who neglects his sword—unprepared when the battle comes. Daniel's discipline in prayer was not just a habit but the anchor that kept him firm in a godless culture. If your life feels unstable, ask yourself: Have you neglected the presence of God? Have you allowed the distractions of life to steal the time that should be devoted to the One who sustains you?

Beyond the spiritual, a man must also steward his body. Strength is not just about the mind and spirit; it includes the vessel God has given him. Neglecting health leads to exhaustion, which weakens leadership. A man lacking energy cannot give his best to his family, work, or mission. Taking care of his body is not about vanity but readiness. A weary king cannot fight effectively. The physical and spiritual are connected; discipline in one area strengthens the other.

One of the greatest threats to a king's focus is distraction. The world offers endless noise—social media, entertainment, instant gratification—all designed to keep men passive and detached from purpose. What a man consumes shapes his heart. Job said, *"I made a covenant with my eyes not to look lustfully at a woman"* (Job 31:1). If Job, without modern technology, had to make that commitment, how much more does a man today need to guard his eyes, his mind, and his time? Every unchecked habit, every indulgence in distractions, is a step away from purpose. A king does not allow himself to be mastered by anything other than his calling.

Growth is not just about personal success—it is about legacy. David prepared resources for a temple he would never see built because he understood that true kings think generationally. A selfish man seeks personal gain; a wise man invests in what will outlive him. What are you building that will endure beyond your lifetime? Will your children inherit wisdom or regret? Will your name be associated with strength and godliness or compromise and wasted potential? The greatest leaders never stop learning. The moment a man believes he has nothing left to learn, he disqualifies himself from future authority. Even at the end of his life, Paul did not boast about his accomplishments; he said, *"I have fought the good fight, I have finished the race, I have kept the faith"* (2 Timothy 4:7). He did not say he had arrived—only that he had remained faithful to the journey.

A king's strength is not in his title but in his endurance. He does not stop seeking, does not stop refining, and does not stop pressing forward. He always maintains a teachable spirit. His mind remains sharp, his spirit remains hungry, and his heart remains humble. He does not wait for hardship to remind him of his need for growth—he chooses to grow every single day. He is not reactive; he is proactive. He does not drift; he builds. And because of that, his reign will not be fleeting but will leave a lasting impact.

The call is clear: Will you remain where you are, or will you rise? A king's choices determine the course of his kingdom. Choose growth. Choose wisdom. Choose to press forward, no matter the cost. Your legacy depends on it.

CLOSING THOUGHTS

A true king never stops growing. He recognises that past victories do not guarantee future faithfulness, and complacency is a quiet threat to his leadership. Driven by discipline rather than fleeting emotion, he remains vigilant through ongoing spiritual intimacy and wise stewardship of his body and mind. He welcomes accountability, knowing that isolation fosters self-deception. Ultimately, a king's commitment to continuous refinement shapes not only his present but also his legacy.

CALL TO ACTION

Refuse to settle for comfort—seek growth relentlessly. Invite accountability into your life, protect your intimacy with God, and steward your physical health so you are always ready to lead. Do not allow distractions or complacency to rob you of your purpose. Choose to press forward, day after day, for the sake of your kingdom and the generations to come.

CHAPTER 22

LEADING AND SERVING IN THE MARKETPLACE

The call to kingship does not end at the threshold of your home or church. A man's influence is shaped by how he conducts himself in the workplace. Biblical leadership principles remain the same whether you hold a high-ranking title, manage a small team, or serve behind the scenes. You were never meant to compartmentalise your faith from your daily work; you are commissioned to embody Christ-like authority and servanthood wherever you earn your living. Colossians 3:23 instructs believers to do their work "as for the Lord, and not for men," revealing that every job, no matter how mundane or glamorous, can become a Kingdom assignment.

A central aspect of leading like a king in your workplace is understanding that your position—boss, supervisor, or staff—is an opportunity to serve. Jesus, the King of kings, consistently displayed servant leadership (Mark 10:45), washing the disciples' feet and caring for their needs. He never leveraged His status for personal gain but stooped low to elevate others. Translating this into the corporate or vocational sphere means treating subordinates, coworkers, and clients with dignity and respect. It means using whatever authority you have to empower them. When mistakes occur, you correct graciously; when successes arise, you celebrate collectively. Authority becomes a tool for building people up rather than exerting power over them.

True servanthood walks hand in hand with excellence and unwavering leadership. A kingly approach to work demands setting high standards for yourself first. Strive to maintain integrity in all dealings—no cutting corners, no bending ethical rules. Demonstrate consistency between what you say in your faith community and what you do on Monday morning. You honour God and your workplace by modelling diligence, punctuality, and reliability. People notice a man who holds himself accountable to higher moral standards, and such a witness often paves the way for deeper conversations about faith. Your exemplary performance bolsters the credibility of your spiritual testimony, showing that Kingdom principles can coexist with real-world success.

The reality is that every workplace hosts its share of conflicts and challenges: stressed colleagues, office politics, or pressures to compromise. A king under Christ's rule confronts these issues head-on with wisdom and grace. Rather than spreading gossip or fuelling negativity, he seeks to mediate peace. Rather than hoarding solutions, he mentors and collaborates, believing that a rising tide lifts all boats. Should injustice surface, he handles it as a modern-day prophet would—calling out unethical practices with gentleness but unwavering conviction. Ephesians 5:11 reminds us to expose deeds of darkness in our office, which might mean standing against dishonest practices or unfair treatment, even when it costs us popularity or a promotion. Risking comfort for integrity demonstrates a king's heart, focused more on pleasing God than gaining human approval.

Spiritual discipline doesn't stop at home or within the church walls; it follows you into the workplace. The same prayer life that strengthens your role as a husband, father, or leader should also shape your decisions in business. Walk with God throughout your day, pausing for brief, intentional prayers before important calls, meetings, or negotiations. Keep your heart aligned by memorising and applying Scriptures like James 1:5, which promises wisdom to those who ask in faith. But don't let your prayers revolve solely around your success. Pray for your coworkers, clients, or superiors—anyone carrying unseen burdens. When you lead with spiritual awareness and compassion, you reflect the heart of a true king—one who sees people not as problems to solve or assets to use but as souls to nurture.

Finally, never forget that your workplace leadership is a living testimony. You may be the only reflection of Christ some people ever see. While you cannot force faith upon anyone, your conduct can spark curiosity about the God you serve. Ask questions about colleagues' families or personal challenges; show compassion when they are overwhelmed. Offer prayer when they face a crisis— often, even non-believers appreciate the genuine concern. In all these acts, you quietly sow seeds of the gospel. Like Daniel, who prospered in a foreign court while maintaining unwavering devotion, you become a beacon of Kingdom values in an environment that is sometimes hostile to them.

Leading as a king in the workplace marries servanthood with resolute leadership. You inspire excellence by example, cultivate healthy relationships marked by kindness, uphold ethical convictions without compromise, and shine the light of Christ in routine tasks as well as critical decisions. That is the essence of a man who understands his broader calling: not merely to succeed by the world's yardstick but to bring God's presence into boardrooms, break rooms, and every space in between. Such a man, anchored in faith and driven by love, will inevitably shape the culture around him—one conversation, one project, one act of integrity at a time.

CLOSING THOUGHTS

As a man called to embody biblical leadership, your influence in the workplace is far-reaching. Following Christ's example means serving others rather than wielding authority for personal gain. It means cultivating integrity, setting the standard of excellence, and addressing challenges with wisdom and grace. By blending servant leadership with decisive action, you become a living testimony, transforming office culture through kindness, moral conviction, and genuine concern for others.

CALL TO ACTION

This week, invite the Holy Spirit into your daily tasks. Make a conscious effort to pray for your colleagues, seek ways to assist or mentor them, and stand for what is right, even when it costs you. Be punctual, fair, and reliable in all you do, reflecting Christ's character through excellence. Determine to use your influence for the Kingdom, empowering those around you and shining God's light in every corner of your workplace.

CHAPTER 23

SERVING COMMUNITIES

A king's influence must extend beyond his home. Too often, men confine their faith and leadership to private spaces, as if their calling is limited to what happens within their four walls. But true kingship demands stepping into the world and shaping it with God's authority. Jesus called His followers to be the salt of the earth and the light of the world—not hidden, not timid, but actively engaging and transforming the culture around them.

The greatest leaders in Scripture were not men who stayed comfortable. Joseph rose from slavery to govern Egypt, not for his personal gain but to save countless lives. Daniel thrived in a pagan empire, refusing to compromise his faith while earning the trust of kings. Nehemiah saw the broken walls of Jerusalem and took action, refusing to stand idly by while his people suffered. Likewise, the world today is in desperate need of godly men who will stand in the gap—men who will mentor, lead, and protect their communities from the chaos of moral and spiritual decline.

A king is not a bystander; he is a builder. He sees the needs around him and refuses to look away. He does not pass the responsibility to someone else or wait for the government, the church, or another leader to step in. He rises. He takes ownership. He moves.

A KING'S CALL TO INFLUENCE

Every man has a sphere of influence, whether at work, in his neighbourhood, or within his extended family. The question is not whether you have influence but whether you are using it for God's purposes. The world teaches men to prioritise personal success, financial gain, and social status. But a king in Christ understands that true leadership is about impact, not image. It is about serving, not self-promotion. Your community should be different because you are in it. Your workplace should operate with more integrity because you are there. Your children's school should have a stronger moral foundation because you speak up.

It is time to stop compartmentalising faith. Sunday morning is not the only sacred space; your workplace, your friendships, and your leadership in community initiatives all matter. Joseph did not lead only in the presence of other believers; he governed a pagan nation with wisdom and integrity. Daniel did not compromise his convictions to fit in with Babylonian culture; he remained faithful while serving in a foreign land. Likewise, you are called to be a man who walks boldly in the world without becoming of the world.

RAISING THE NEXT GENERATION

Legacy is not what you leave behind when you die; it is what you build while you live. Younger men are watching you, whether you realise it or not. They are observing how you handle conflict, how you treat women, how you respond to pressure, and how seriously you take your faith. Many young men today are growing up without strong father figures, leaving them vulnerable to cultural confusion about identity, manhood, and purpose. But God has positioned you to stand in the gap, to model stability, discipline, and wisdom.

Paul mentored Timothy, calling him his "true son in the faith." He did not wait for Timothy to figure things out alone; he guided, equipped, and encouraged him to stand firm. This is what the next generation needs, not lectures from a distance, but fathers and mentors who will invest time, energy, and wisdom into shaping them into strong, godly men.

Mentorship does not require perfection. You do not have to have all the answers to guide someone younger than you. What is needed is availability, honesty, and a willingness to walk alongside them. Be the example that breaks cycles of passivity and confusion. Show them what authentic manhood looks like—steadfast, honourable, and deeply rooted in faith.

STANDING FOR TRUTH IN A COMPROMISED CULTURE

The world is shifting. Moral relativism, fatherlessness, and identity crisis are eroding the foundation of families and communities. Many men shrink back in the face of cultural pressure, afraid of backlash or rejection. But a king does not cower. He stands. He speaks. He leads.

Daniel was taken captive to Babylon, where the entire system was designed to re-educate him away from his faith. Yet he refused to compromise, choosing to remain faithful in prayer, conduct, and convictions. He did not rage against the culture in anger or surrender to it in fear. He stood firm, and in doing so, he transformed the hearts of kings.

A king's voice matters. Do not be afraid to stand up for biblical values in your workplace, your children's schools, or in the public arena. But do so with wisdom, grace, and unwavering conviction. Truth spoken in anger often falls on deaf ears, but truth spoken in love has the power to change hearts. Engage with those who disagree, not to win arguments but to win souls. The goal is not to defeat people in debate but to reflect Christ in every conversation.

A CALL TO ACTION

Your leadership is needed now more than ever. This world does not need more passive men who remain silent while families, communities, and generations suffer. It needs kings, men who take action, pray with boldness, mentor the fatherless, protect the weak, and serve with conviction. The time for waiting is over. The time for stepping into your God-given authority is now.

Your community is waiting. Your workplace is waiting. The next generation is waiting. Will you rise? Will you stand? Will you lead? The answer is not in your words but in your actions. A king does not wait for permission to build. He sees the need and starts the work.

CLOSING THOUGHTS

You have walked through the fires of self-discovery, wrestled with the weight of responsibility, and embraced the call to kingship. This journey was never meant to be easy, nor was it designed for the faint of heart. A king is not crowned in comfort, he is forged in the trials, decisions, and sacrifices that shape his legacy. But now, standing at this threshold, you must ask yourself: Will I carry this mantle forward, or will I let it slip through my fingers?

True kingship is not about a one-time awakening but a lifetime of refinement. The world will tempt you to settle, grow complacent, and exchange your authority for mediocrity. Do not let that be your story. A man of God does not drift, he anchors himself in truth, disciplines his body and mind, and governs his household and community with unwavering conviction. This is your final charge: to live, lead, and love with the strength, wisdom, and honour of the King who first called you.

Your story is not finished. The greatest chapters are yet to be written. Stand firm, move forward, and let your life be a testament to what it means to reign under the authority of Christ. The world is watching, your family is counting on you, and the Kingdom needs you to rise. **Now go forth, king.** The world is waiting for the authentic you to rise and lead.

CHAPTER 24

GO FORTH AND CONQUER IN CHRIST'S AUTHORITY

You started this journey maybe unsure, wounded, or curious. You've wrestled with tough questions, confronted inner barriers, embraced accountability, and learned to see yourself through the lens of Scripture. A royal priest with dominion to shape culture, bless families, and restore communities. Now, you stand on a threshold: either revert to comfortable passivity or walk through the open door of perpetual growth and lasting legacy.

The choice is yours. But remember that the same Holy Spirit who empowered biblical heroes dwells in you. He's not stingy with His anointing nor limited by your weaknesses. He delights in using ordinary men like fishermen, shepherds, and tax collectors—to accomplish extraordinary things. Why not you?

As you close this final part, let the words of Joshua 1:9 echo in your subconscious, reshaping your mindset: *"Be strong and courageous. Do not be afraid; do not be discouraged, for the Lord your God will be with you wherever you go."* That promise still stands. Carry it in your heart, your actions, and your prayers. Step forward, King—armed with the truth, fortified by grace and determined to see God's Kingdom advance on every front you touch.

Your story isn't over. It's just beginning to unfold in its greatest chapters. May you press on, relentlessly curious, humbly confident, and wholeheartedly surrender to the glorious reign of Christ in and through your life. Go forth and live the legacy you were destined to leave.

Your crown is not for mere decoration; it's a symbol of purpose, responsibility, and divine calling. As you set this book aside, never forget: your life story is still unfolding. You're writing a narrative with your choices, priorities, and relationships. God has graced you with authority, not to dominate, but to bless. Take your place among the men who refuse to drift. Stand firm, fight well, and leave a legacy that testifies to the grandeur of God's Kingdom.

ACKNOWLEDGEMENTS

To the King of kings, whose wisdom is eternal, whose grace restores, and whose voice has summoned this message into being. May this book serve as a vessel of His divine order returning to the earth.

To every man who longs for truth, chooses righteousness through Christ, and hears the call to rise into kingship, may you lead with strength, serve with humility, and reign with divine wisdom.

To the men who were never shown what true kingship looks like—may this book be your compass in the fog, a battle cry in the silence, and a reminder that kingship is not inherited by blood but forged through truth, tested in fire, and shaped by faith.

To my beloved grandmother, Naomi Jonker, and my precious children, Lanae and Lukas—your love, encouragement, and quiet strength have upheld me more than you know. This book carries your imprint as much as my own. You are my legacy and my reason.

To my Pastor, Erik van Rhyn, and my unofficial mentor, Lizane van Aarde, your unwavering obedience to God, wisdom, and bold leadership have marked my journey deeply. This work stands because of the foundation you laid. I honour you with deep gratitude.

ABOUT THE AUTHOR

Anke Mostert is a devoted mother of two from Somerset West, Cape Town. Her journey, marked by the highs of motherhood and the deep valleys of nearly a decade-long marriage that ended in divorce, ignited a powerful awakening. In the stillness after the storm, Anke came to see the world for what it truly is and, more importantly, to recognise the root cause of its brokenness.

Anke pours her heart into her calling—relationship, identity, and purpose coaching—driven by a fierce love for people. She walks beside individuals and couples with balanced tenderness and tenacity, healing rifts, rebuilding trust, and exposing the latent gold of God-given passions and strengths within. By steering clients toward their True North, she ignites wholeness and influence that ripples through every sphere of life.

Drawing from her time in the United Kingdom, where she worked with individuals from diverse backgrounds, Anke brings a rich perspective shaped by experience in the beauty industry, holistic healing, and transformational coaching. She has led numerous workshops and personal development sessions, blending empathy with empowerment and always guiding from a place of authentic connection.

For Anke, this book is more than words—it's an urgent call to establish God's divine order on earth, an invitation to step into a life of alignment, clarity, true identity and Kingdom purpose.

DISCLAIMER

King—Your Call to Rise was birthed from a deep well of personal transformation, spiritual insight, and a desire to awaken the royal identity within men. Every message, design, and word is crafted intentionally to inspire, heal, and remind men of their God-given authority, worth, and purpose. I stand fully behind the message of Kingship, not just as a Kingdom ambassador, but as one who has lived, wrestled with, and walked through the very truths it carries.

The content shared in the King—Your Call To Rise book, its teachings, and the accompanying brand materials are intended for personal growth, inspiration, and spiritual reflection. This is not a substitute for licensed therapy, clinical counselling, or professional medical advice. While the messages are faith-based and deeply personal, they are shared from lived experience, not as professional, medical or psychological guidance. Any actions taken and/or decisions made by engaging with this material are the sole responsibility of the reader.

www.ingramcontent.com/pod-product-compliance
Lightning Source LLC
Chambersburg PA
CBHW031134090426
42738CB00008B/1083